BRYAN REIMER & MAGNUS LINDKVIST

HOW TO MAKE AI USEFUL

MOVING BEYOND THE HYPE TO REAL PROGRESS IN **BUSINESS**, **SOCIETY** AND **LIFE**

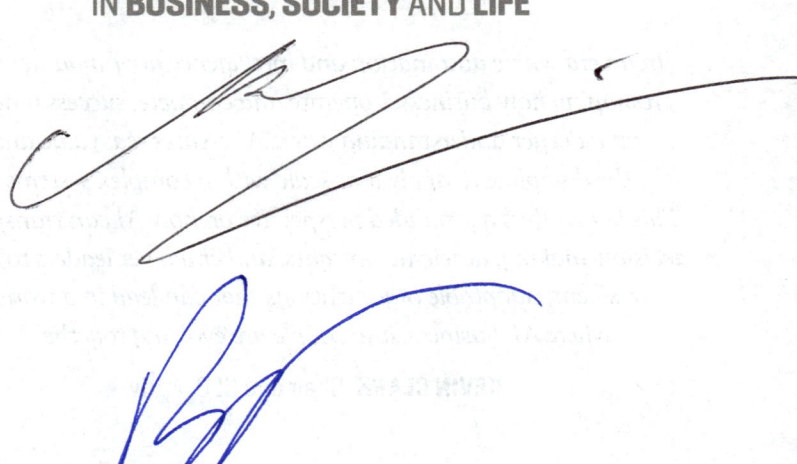

ADVANCE PRAISE

"A must-read for anyone looking to unlock the true value of AI—in business, policy, or everyday life.

This book tells a compelling story about human-centric AI through the unique perspectives of a pragmatic possibilitist and a futurist. Drawing on real-world case studies, it explores how accelerated AI innovation and the technologies it enables are reshaping the systems we live in and depend on.

At its core is a quietly provocative question: 'Will we let AI change us?'—a challenge that is as underappreciated as it is urgent. In a time when we must focus on humanizing technology before it dehumanizes us, this book offers a thoughtful, grounded, and timely guide for navigating what comes next."

RANA EL KALIOUBY, PhD, Co-Founder and Managing Partner, Blue Tulip Ventures; Co-Founder and CEO, Affectiva

"In an era where automation and intelligence are fundamentally reshaping how businesses operate and compete, success hinges on a deeper understanding where AI creates real value and the discipline to apply it at scale within complex systems. This book offers a grounded perspective on how AI can transform decision-making, accelerate insights, and empower leaders to build resilient, adaptable organizations that can lead in a world where AI, business, and people are evolving together."

KEVIN CLARK, Chair and CEO, Aptiv

"This is a delightful book on AI whose primary purpose is neither 'selling' nor 'denouncing' AI. By using an abundance of real-world examples, both historical and personal, the authors explore the space where we humans meet AI. While this is about AI, the book is about us, as we often find the promise of AI both thrilling and unsettling. This is a practical guide to how industries, societies, and consumers can choose to use AI, instead of being mesmerized or intimidated by AI's technological advances."

JUNKO YOSHIDA, Editor-in-Chief, *Junko's Tech Probe* (https://junkoyoshidaparis.substack.com/), former Global Editor-in-Chief at *EE Times*

"AI's true revolution isn't in its algorithms, but in how we apply them. Reimer and Lindkvist illuminate the path from technological wow to practical progress—making this essential reading for anyone seeking to transform tomorrow's promise into today's reality."

JOSEPH COUGHLIN, Founder and Director, MIT AgeLab; Author of *The Longevity Economy*

"*As a researcher with over a decade of experience staying close to the leading edge of AI's development, I found this book to be a refreshing departure from the familiar polarized view on optimist vs. pessimist AI futures. Rather than speculating on final outcomes, it focuses on a more immediate and pressing challenge: how to make it work for us in a practical sense, today.*

The ample and thoroughly entertaining metaphors and historical parallels drawn in the book frame AI not merely as a technical artifact but as part of a broader sociotechnical system. These narrative elements— rare in academic discourse—provide a compelling counterbalance to the abstraction and reductionism often found in research literature.

How to Make AI Useful isn't about the next breakthrough model or benchmark. It's about the systems-level thinking, human factors, and institutional realities we too often overlook in the pursuit of state-of-the-art performance. A timely, articulate reflection on where AI is—and where it needs to go."

MAURICIO MUÑOZ, Senior Research Engineer, AI Sweden

"Accidental writing duo Bryan Reimer and Magnus Lindkvist dodge the danger of writing a quickly outdated book on AI by making an apt comparison with the rise of electricity a century ago. They make clear with many examples how the bubble of the balloon can be distinguished in the different stages of innovations. And they reassure the reader with logic that creativity remains human: 'embracing imperfection and transforming life's uncertainty into something meaningful.'"

MARTIJN LOFVERS, Serial entrepreneur and author who developed a knowledge base with machine learning and AI at Supply Chain Media and applies a GenAI tool for strategic scenario building as Co-Founder of Supply Chain Companions

"How to Make AI Useful *offers an engaging look at how artificial intelligence may change the way we live and work. Reimer's seminal work on human-machine teamwork, especially in self-driving cars, seems to offer profound lessons for how to work alongside increasingly powerful AI systems most effectively. With Lindkvist's blending of real-world examples to challenge how we think about the future, the book offers a refreshingly clear picture of where AI is taking us, and how we should adapt."

WILL KNIGHT, Senior writer, WIRED

Published by
LID Publishing
An imprint of LID Business Media Ltd.
LABS House, 15-19 Bloomsbury Way,
London, WC1A 2TH, UK

info@lidpublishing.com
www.lidpublishing.com

A member of:
BPR
businesspublishersroundtable.com

All rights reserved. Without limiting the rights under copyright reserved, no part of this publication may be reproduced, stored or introduced into a retrieval system, or transmitted, in any form or by any means (electronic, mechanical, photocopying, recording or otherwise) without the prior written permission of both the copyright owners and the publisher of this book.

© Bryan Reimer and Magnus Lindkvist, 2025
© LID Business Media Limited, 2025
Reprinted in 2025

Printed and bound in Great Britain by Halstan Ltd

ISBN: 978-1-917391-48-1
ISBN: 978-1-917391-49-8 (ebook)

Cover and page design: Caroline Li

BRYAN REIMER & MAGNUS LINDKVIST

HOW TO MAKE AI USEFUL

MOVING BEYOND THE HYPE TO REAL PROGRESS
IN **BUSINESS, SOCIETY** AND **LIFE**

LID

MADRID | MEXICO CITY | LONDON
BUENOS AIRES | BOGOTA | SHANGHAI

BRYAN:
To my family—Kim, Cary, Lynn, Sierra, Brooke, Nolan, and Ellie—who continue to shape me every day. To my colleagues, Joe and Bruce, together with countless others, supporters, and collaborators who have helped me become who I am. With sincere appreciation to Magnus, who helped craft this amazing journey!

MAGNUS:
Dedicated to anyone who spends their day
creating something.
That includes my co-pilot on this project.
Thank you, Bryan!

CONTENTS

Prelude: A Wild Ride   2
Introduction: From Hype to Progress   8

PART 1: WOW!   30
Chapter One: AI as a Doer   32
Chapter Two: AI as an Assistant   72
Chapter Three: AI as a Creator   104

PART 2: WHOA!   136
Chapter Four: Will We Let AI Change Us?   138

PART 3: GROW!   162
Chapter Five: Patching in The Tactical Phase   164
Chapter Six: Paving in The Strategic Phase   194

Outro: Onwards, Upwards, and Outwards   226

Endnotes   242
Acknowledgments   252

Photo Credit: Johan Bergmark

BEFORE WE BEGIN, THE 'I' IN OUR AI BOOK

This is a co-authored book, but in order to not confuse the reader with too many perspectives, we've written it from the point of view of Bryan. Think of us as the Pet Shop Boys, an English pop group, where Magnus is Chris Lowe behind the synthesizer and Bryan is Neil Tennant behind the microphone. That, at least, was the brief we gave to our photographer.

PRELUDE
A WILD RIDE

A parking lot somewhere in Las Vegas, January 2018.

It was just before the opening of CES, the annual technology exhibition known for showing off various gadgets from all corners of the globe. I was in a car, and it was driving itself. Not assistive driving. Not remote control. An actual self-driving car. Albeit surrounded by a few humans ready to intervene if the technology went haywire.

I had spent some years at MIT, deep-diving into the realm of autonomous vehicles and founding several initiatives[1] working to optimize driver–vehicle interfaces and safety systems. I had just begun working with several global efforts, laying out the opportunities and challenges that the coming age of self-driving vehicles would present. I had spoken at academic and industry conferences and with countless industry executives and government officials. I had read papers and contributed to them. But I hadn't been inside an operational, 'self-driving' vehicle before. Not until now. On a clear, crisp morning in a sealed-off parking lot outside the Las Vegas Convention Center. With a back-up safety driver and engineer in the front seat, I sat in the rear.

All I could think, and feel, was: Wow!

The technology had leaped.

And my mind started to wander.

What exactly is this thing, Wow!?

Driving is not one precise activity.

Sometimes, it's a logistical exercise of transporting somebody and something from point A to point B. A commute. A shipment. A delivery. Functional driving or just a stroll out for ice cream.

Sometimes, driving is a valve to let off steam. We use the daily commute to let our minds wander or work through situations or dilemmas. Or listen to golden oldies on the stereo. Or catch up on podcasts. Or check the news headlines.

Sometimes, we let others drive us for comfort, status, or necessity.

At other times, we floor the gas pedal to see what this baby can really do.

We watch others floor the gas pedal and compete in NASCAR or Formula One.

We slam the door shut, get in our car, and just drive away—from an argument, from heartbreak, or from our parents who don't understand what we are going through.

We make our memories in the car. We even make love in the car.

We cry and laugh.

We socialize and meditate.

For some, the car is the office; for others, the car is the third place between home and work, where we eat, and even take a nap (hopefully not while driving). Possibly get a full night's sleep if the back seats can be folded down or the summer cottage is just a bit too cramped for all of us.

When we say a car is self-driving, we don't mean a vehicle that will do everything for us. We are pointing to a new technological frontier—one that can handle some tasks and assist us with others.

Most importantly, we are venturing into uncharted territory.

A seemingly magical force tamed by humans.

A dream of a place where everything is different, even better.

A place we call the future.

In a nondescript Las Vegas parking lot on a January morning.

A few years later, in an Uber with my partner racing through Lisbon.

I am starting to panic. I scan the road ahead for red traffic lights and check the door handle lightly to see if it can be opened quickly. I have an urge to escape. Out of the car. And away from the madman who is driving.

Driving is a generous term. Racing with a death wish is more like it.

We have dodged vehicles and pedestrians. Run red lights. Skidded in a sharp turn. All of this well above the legal speed limit and frequently hitting two digits on the speedometer in bumper-to-bumper traffic (European, so kilometers per hour).

I'm late for a VIP dinner at a convention where I've spoken earlier that day. It went well. The audience, consisting primarily of insurance people in the automotive field, seemed inspired and intrigued by the coming age of 'automagical' technology and how it would radically change cars, driving, and vehicular safety for that matter.

Now, I find my heart racing, my breath shallow, and my life almost flashing before my eyes as a Portuguese Uber driver is hellbent on killing us.

Predicting technology is less complicated than predicting the timeline on which it will arrive.

I find myself wishing that somebody could just shoot some kind of invasive software patch—like a dart—at this car and enable fully autonomous, life-saving driving.

My prayers go unanswered.

My fears, too.

I arrive, alive but sweat-drenched, at the dinner venue.

It is a gorgeous summer evening.

I deserve a glass of red wine. Or two.

A few hours—and more than two glasses of wine—later.

I have been rambling on about how much the world of cars, driving, safety, and insurance will change. I think I've used the words 'disruptive' and 'revolution' about 50 times. The people next to me—various delegates and executives from the event—have been curious, amused, amazed, flabbergasted, and frightened. I'm on a wine-fueled storytelling streak.

That's when Magnus, a fellow speaker at the event, asks me a question.

"So, what do you think of AI?"

He's a tall, Swedish futurologist who has been listening attentively to my musings. As he's not due to speak until the next day (a talk that because of my hectic schedule, I couldn't even stay for), he's stuck to water as his beverage of choice.

Artificial intelligence has, for the past couple of years, been the hype—THE HYPE—in the business and technology world.

Where we once dreamed of fully autonomous cars, we are now dreaming of a fully autonomous world.

Magnus and I start bouncing ideas off each other.

Will we still write? Think? Work? What can AI really do, and what can't it do?

As we're chatting away, I start seeing parallels to what I've spent more than a decade on.

Just like driving, we are talking about living, working, and thriving—not as one thing but as a long list of tasks and activities.

Just like with cars, the vast majority of people don't care—let alone understand—what's underneath the hood.

Just like the century of the automobile gave us suburbs, Bruce Springsteen songs, LA freeways, traffic jams, and radio advertising, the coming century will be full of second-order effects created by all things AI.

The car has always been at the forefront of the question: What's next?

Flying cars. Driverless cars. Small cars. SUVs. Electric, connected, ugly, or beautiful.

Now we humans are at center stage.

How will we change in the face of the automating, facilitating, and assistive technologies that fit under the umbrella of artificial intelligence?

The conversation that started that evening led to the book you are now reading.

Strap in for a wild ride.

INTRODUCTION

FROM HYPE TO PROGRESS

TURBULENCE AND TRANSFORMATION

If the New York Electrical Show had been organized in the 2020s, social media feeds would have overflowed with selfies and videos of cutting-edge gadgets. But this was 1919. Instead of archived Instagram posts, we have an illustration from the long-defunct *The Electrical Experimenter*[2] magazine to glimpse the excitement surrounding electricity, a transformative yet misunderstood technology of the time.

SOURCE: *The Electrical Experimenter*. December, 1919, 761. (https://energyhistory.yale.edu/new-york-electrical-show-illustration-1919/)

Electricity was a novelty, but was it useful? If so, how and for whom? Enthusiasts imagined electric trucks, 'rug washers,' and a curious invention called a 'radio direction finder.' Like today's tech expos unveiling concept cars or foldable LED screens, the Electrical Show overpromised. Glowing bathtubs and washing machines that turned 'wash day' into 'joy day' were fantastical. Even a simple lamp was branded an 'Electrical Vase Light Attachment.'

At the center of this spectacle stood the 'Electricity Fairy,' a scantily clad figure cradling a glowing bulb, immortalized in a mural still on display at the Museum of Modern Art in Paris. This icon captured both the wonder and the absurdity of the era's hype.

Sometimes, the excitement tipped into outright fantasy. One bizarre claim suggested that public school children could be 'improved' through mild electric shocks, citing dubious experiments in Sweden.[3] These ideas, as wild as they were, reflected a society grappling with the promises and pitfalls of a technology it was just beginning to understand.

To understand such bold claims, we must consider the world in which they arose. In 1919, society stood at a crossroads of profound change. The Great War and the Spanish Flu had killed millions, while empires crumbled, replaced by fragile democracies or authoritarian regimes.

Electricity wasn't the only force reshaping the world. Automobiles began transforming cities, and radio revolutionized communication. Old industries, like Hermès' luxury saddle-making business, teetered as horses gave way to cars. Amid this upheaval, people dreamed of a new society but had only fragments of the puzzle.

Art reflected this uncertainty. Movements like Modernism and Fauvism reimagined reality, while scientific breakthroughs, such as the discovery of the atom, provided both awe and existential dread. Russian painter Wassily Kandinsky captured this sense of instability in 1913:

> The crumbling of the atom was to my soul like the crumbling of the whole world ... Suddenly, the heaviest walls toppled. Everything became uncertain, tottering and weak.[4]

In the dreamscapes of these early days, we failed to grasp the reality of what it would be like to one day live with electricity embedded into society. Electricity would sparkle skylines at night, enabling nightshift workers and karaoke bars. It would enable power tools and personal stereos. Refrigerated food and microwave cooking. Escalators and elevators. What we failed to imagine were connected devices, all the brownouts and power grids in disarray. CO_2 emissions. Price hikes and infrastructure budget deficits. Accidents, fires, and fatalities. In our dreams about the future, electricity was something elegant and transformational. In the reality that unfolded, it became messy, complicated, and often dirty. To be sure, it changed the world. But certainly not like we had anticipated at the New York Electrical Show.

IT'S HAPPENING AGAIN

In the early 2020s, researchers at Bain & Company, a consultancy, plotted 175 years of global turbulence, tracking wars, pandemics, financial crises, and climate disasters. The resulting chart shows how turbulence ebbs and flows across history, like the proverbial pendulum. It also shows how the 2020s rank among the most turbulent periods in modern history. The belief that we are living in unprecedented times, it seems, is not just a hunch but a measurable fact.

Paired with the turbulence, a general doom and gloom has swept through the world, creating a zeitgeist of declinism and political turmoil.

Amid this uncertainty, AI has become our modern-day 'Electricity Fairy.' Its potential is hyped to absurdity, and every day brings new headlines about how it will upend industries, make many tasks and job roles obsolete, and change society as we know it. Unfortunately, AI lacks the succinct definition of electricity. Technology writer David Petersson calls it "the simulation of human intelligence by machines," but he adds that

AI's definition is continually evolving as we develop new tools to simulate human capabilities.[5] Larry Tesler, a computer scientist, famously remarked in 1970 that "intelligence is whatever machines haven't done yet."

AI, at its core, is a piece of unpredictable, anthropomorphized software. For some, it is a harbinger of doom, promising to enslave humanity. For others, it's a utopian vision of abundance, where humans are freed from mundane jobs and chores:

> "AI will be the most profound shift of our lifetimes."

> "The largest change to the global labor market in human history."

> "In a decade perhaps everyone on earth will be capable of accomplishing more than the most impactful person can today."[6]

You would be forgiven for thinking that these are delusional cult leaders talking in tongues, but they are prognostications by the CEOs of some of the world's leading companies in the field of AI.

Whatever its future may hold, it has become an economic engine, driving stock market valuations, data center investments, and coffee room conversations.

Over the past few years, investment in AI has skyrocketed, with billions flowing into startups, infrastructure, and research. Major tech firms are pouring unprecedented sums into AI development—Google, Microsoft, and Meta alone are committing over $200 billion to AI-driven infrastructure.[7] Venture capital funding for AI startups now represents a significant share of global investments, reflecting the widespread belief that AI will reshape industries, economies, and human potential. Whether this leads to utopia or upheaval, one thing is clear: AI is no longer just amazing technology—it's an economic force reshaping the world.

As a satirical account on X put it: "Al Qaeda rebrands itself A.I. Qaeda and raises $1 billion in funding."[8]

In this speculative frenzy, a new phenomenon has emerged: FOLO, or the Fear of Losing Out. FOLO grips investors, policymakers, and businesses alike. The rush to secure AI dominance, to pour billions into various AI-driven ventures, and to stake claims on the frontier of automation is as much about fear as it is about ambition. No one wants to be left behind, whether they understand the technology or not.

What matters is not the technical definition of AI but the Rorschach test it presents. Some see limitless progress, others a looming catastrophe. AI is a symbol of wonder and absurdity.

How will we work, live, and thrive in the future? What jobs are safe, if any? How will power be distributed? What will we belong to—tribes, nations, or The Matrix? Who are the enemies?

Author Joanna Maciejewska's aphorism captures our ambiguity perfectly: "I want AI to do my laundry and dishes so that I can do art and writing, not for AI to do my art and writing so that I can do my laundry and dishes."[9]

DUDE, WHERE'S MY UTILITY?

Lovable, Granola, Perplexity, Cubby, Codeium, Rosebud, Curio. These could easily be mistaken for pet names, recreational drugs, or perfume brands. Yet they are examples of the exponentially growing list of AI-enabled services and platforms already populated by ChatGPT, DeepSeek, CoPilot, and Claude. The services span a bewildering array of offerings, from generative text tools, no-code build-anything platforms, and personalized health coaches to AI-powered girlfriends and compliance-monitoring tools.

The cascade of new ideas is as inspiring as it is confusing. The hyperbolic rhetoric distorts. Much of AI's current appeal is wrapped in spin.

The term 'artificial intelligence' is perhaps best understood as a marketing slogan that emerges whenever technological capability outpaces human imagination. From this point of view, artificial intelligence is a pipe dream about making computers do what they do in the movies, and the dreams-and-nightmares factory is in full swing, with job-stealing doom-mongers alongside videos of dancing spaghetti or fake images of the Pope in a puffer jacket. This phase is typical of the early years of an emerging technology wherein the potential utility is obscured by novelty.

When the mobile phone was new, it was not particularly mobile. Nokia's Mobira Talkman looked more like a small petrol canister than a cellphone and was 'mobile' in name only. The Motorola DynaTAC cost thousands of dollars in the 1980s, and calls were so expensive that the most common thing people did was bragging that they could now make (very short) phone calls from their car.

Or consider the early dot-com boom when e-commerce was marketed as enabling you to 'shop naked.' Like many AI-powered gimmicks, this fetishized idea was not solving an underserved need but merely hyping the novelty value of a new technology. Some graffiti seen in London at the time summarized it well: "The Internet—lots of porn and free music but what else?"

Tools don't revolutionize the world—mindsets do. Technology may advance at the speed of Moore's Law, doubling its power every two years, but cultural and mindset shifts happen much more slowly. Minds change at the speed of generational turnover, often requiring decades (and sometimes lots of education) to adapt to new paradigms. Besides, 'useful' means different things to different people.

... IT DEPENDS ON WHO'S ASKING

Because AI is so broad in its scope and has the potential to affect all aspects of life, it's helpful to consider the diversity of people involved and their perspectives. At one end of the spectrum, we find the corporate sector, where profits are the lifeblood, and longevity depends on successful business development and innovation. Incumbent companies often prioritize doing their existing business better rather than risking money on unproven ventures. This tendency explains why the Fortune 500 list changes so dramatically from decade to decade as new technologies disrupt old business models.

On the other end of the spectrum, we have politicians who view the world through the lens of the three Rs: risk, regulation, and reelection. Between these poles, we encounter smaller players, such as researchers and developers, who explore the frontiers of AI and tackle its technical challenges. These individuals can sometimes fall prey to 'engineeringitis,' where a technically elegant solution endlessly searches for a real-world problem to solve. The application of research in products with impact on society is too frequently viewed as someone else's problem.

Investors, meanwhile, are opportunistic and will join any ride that promises to generate alpha—a fancy term for excess returns on investment. They enthusiastically cheer on trends as long as the arrows point upward but quickly distance themselves when market conditions inevitably turn sour.

Then there are consumers, who, it has been said, are ultimately interested in three things: money, sex, or fame. We shop for deals to save money, invest in clothes or makeup to enhance attractiveness and post selfies on Instagram to gain followers. Consumer tastes are volatile and restless, but if AI can provide an advantage or a thrill for the average Joe or Joanne, it will capture their money or attention.

Finally, we have AI-focused NGOs and activists who, like the proverbial person with a hammer, see every problem as a nail. Their perspectives often dominate debates, but they, too, represent just one piece of a multifaceted puzzle.

Understanding these diverse perspectives is crucial, but so is understanding where we, the authors, are coming from. We are neither evangelists nor alarmists. Instead, we approach AI as Pragmatic Possibilists—balancing curiosity with realism, speculation with evidence.

From the US tech frontier to Sweden's slower adoption curve, our backgrounds shape how we analyze AI's unfolding impact.

ENTER THE PRAGMATIC POSSIBILISTS

I am Dr Bryan Reimer, a Research Scientist at the MIT Center for Transportation and Logistics and MIT AgeLab. I have over two decades invested in studying automotive technology and a decade of experience at the intersection of technology, business, and public policy of automated vehicles, which has long been at the forefront of humankind's quest to automate tasks using emerging digital tools. It has taught me to be skeptical of hype and to respect our inability to accurately predict timelines—'when' things will happen as opposed to 'what.' Being surrounded by some of the world's foremost technology experts in and around MIT has taught me to be a master interpreter of *their* interpretations of the future and finding the signal between the noise.

I'm an avid skier and spend my free time away from research and lectures on the ski slopes of New England, coaching new and experienced ski racers to glide on all forms of frozen water.

My co-author and co-pilot, Magnus Lindkvist, is a generalist futurologist from Sweden—a fox, not a hedgehog.

He thrives on connecting seemingly unrelated ideas, blending stories from business, science, and the arts to spot emerging trends. In 2020, he was asked by *Dagens Industri*, Sweden's most prominent business daily, to make 10 predictions about the year 2021, ranging from stock market performance to sports results. A year later, the verdict was in. He had made one accurate prediction. But true to my insight about timelines, four years later, five more of his predictions had come true, including a Nobel Prize to AlphaFold. The 'when' is a more significant prediction challenge than the 'what.' Bear that in mind as you read our book.

What united us beyond the wine-fueled Lisbon evening is a shared curiosity about the future tempered by pragmatism. Neither utopians nor dystopians, we aim to explore the practical implications of AI, cutting through the hype to ask: What does this technology mean for society in the years ahead?

We come from two very different AI worlds: my home, the United States, is a global AI superpower, while Magnus's Sweden is a country still searching for its place in the AI race. The USA consistently ranks first in the Global AI Index, with its tech industry dominating the global stage. As Palantir CEO Dr Alex Karp declared:

> America is in the very beginning of a revolution that we own—the AI revolution. We own it. It should basically be called the 'US AI Revolution.' Every relevant tech company in the world is here. There is no other place to do technology at scale besides America.[10]

Meanwhile, Sweden has seen its AI ranking fall out of the top 20 in the 2020s, now trailing behind countries like Saudi Arabia and Italy and lacking both significant investment levels and visionary acumen.

By blending two contrasting perspectives, the book draws from both ends of the AI spectrum: the USA, where AI-driven businesses are reshaping industries at breakneck speed, and Sweden, where the momentum is slower. This approach ensures a more balanced, global view—reflecting both tech-driven ambition and human-centered caution.

While I have published hundreds of scientific peer-reviewed articles, this book is not about pure scientific research and should not be interpreted as an academic textbook or a journal article. Scientists tend to use words like 'can and may,' whereas we will go out on a limb and use words like 'will' and 'shall.' Think of it as a playful rough guide to a rapidly evolving field.

This book is not about distant fantasies or cautionary tales of robot overlords. It is about the messy and fascinating task of making sense of a transformative technology as it unfolds. While the future remains uncertain, combining pragmatism with possibility offers the best path forward. Dreams and nightmares about new technology are entertaining, but the question this book seeks to answer is more straightforward: Is AI useful? How? For whom? What steps are needed to make everyone everywhere a part of the AI transformation long after the bubble inevitably bursts?

CLARIFYING OUR DEFINITION OF AI

Before we dive deeper, let's clarify what we mean by 'AI' in the context of this book. Technically speaking, artificial intelligence refers to the algorithms and computational techniques enabling machines to perform tasks that typically require human intelligence. However, our exploration goes beyond mere algorithms and into something broader—AI as advanced technologies and systems enabled by these algorithms.

In other words, when we discuss AI, we encompass not only the code and methods themselves but also the practical applications, products, services, infrastructures and human experiences built around and powered by these algorithms. Our narrative thus reflects a holistic, pragmatic approach to AI, examining how these systems shape—and will continue to shape—societies, businesses, and individual lives.

BUBBLES AND BALLOONS: BOOM, BUST THEN BUILD

The Electrical Show was not the starting point of the electrical revolution. In fact, from Benjamin Franklin's famous experiments and Italy's Alessandro Volta inventing the battery to Faraday and Henry's primitive electrical motor, the 1919 Show bookended a century of electrical experimentation. There had even been a speculative financial bubble at the turn of the century. But electricity itself was not a bubble, but a balloon.

Balloons and bubbles look the same. Both are round and float upwards. But when bubbles pop, they disappear. Balloons can pop, but they can also deflate, sink for a while, and then get reinflated. When the merger mania and outlandish stock market valuations of electricity companies in the late 1800s fizzled out, the inventions and wires were still in place, ready for productive use. Similarly, after a decade of irrational exuberance in railway investments in the late 1800s, the US railway system was bankrupt, but the tracks were still there for future players to use. The dot.com bubble destroyed billions of dollars in market cap, but the fiber optic cables were installed underground, ready for the next wave of digital trickery. To put it in the words of Byrne Hobart and Tobias Huber, who have studied the long-term utility of financial bubbles:

> At the core of an innovation-accelerating bubble is a definite vision of the future that drives extreme commitment from investors and other participants. A bubble can be a collective delusion but also an expression of collective vision.[11]

History doesn't repeat itself, but it rhymes, echoes, and snaps into patterns. The AI bubble will burst—an inevitable phase in the lifecycle of transformative technologies—and the 2020s may very well mark the dramatic end of AI's first overhyped chapter, as the technology (or, more accurately, family of technologies) stumbles under the weight of its promises. Yet, as history shows, disillusionment often fertilizes the ground for true innovation. From the ashes of exaggerated expectations, AI's real potential will emerge—a phoenix rising to usher in a new era of utility and transformation.

THE THREE PHASES FROM NOVELTY TO UTILITY

The journey from the pzazz of phase 1 to the societal progress of phase 3 is not guaranteed; it tends to be long and winding and significantly messier than originally envisioned. More importantly, the companies and nations that dominate one phase may not dominate the next. Sweden and Finland dominated mobile phones with Ericsson and Nokia, respectively, in the late 1990s. A decade later, the USA and South Korea had taken over. Similarly, Stanley Motor Carriage Company, Duesenberg, Panhard and NSU were American, French and German car brands who saw their market share erode and disappear as the sector evolved in the 20th century.

In AI, the Wow! phase is dominated by American and Chinese players because it suits the relatively unregulated, capitalist free-for-all of the U.S. or the fast-learning copycat culture in China.

This does not mean that Chinese or American companies are well suited to revolutionize healthcare systems in Europe, schools in Africa, or factories across Asia.

WE SEE THREE DISTINCT PHASES UNFOLDING BEFORE US.

	Phase 1: "Wow!" → Novelty (Discovery & Hype)	**Phase 2:** "Whoa!" → Disruption (Utility & Transformation)	**Phase 3:** "Grow!" → Maturity (Optimization & Integration)
Characteristics	• A surge of new ideas, gadgets, and technological wizardry. • Demos and experiments generate excitement, often exceeding real-world readiness. • Early adopters explore possibilities, sometimes in unrealistic or speculative ways.	• AI enters real-world environments—organizations, schools, and industries. • Practical challenges emerge: integration issues, ethical dilemmas, and institutional resistance. • Unintended consequences surface; we realize that we've overlooked key factors. • 'Patching' becomes necessary—adjusting policies, workflows, and expectations.	• AI becomes a foundational utility—ubiquitous, reliable, and seamlessly integrated. • Like electricity or paved roads, it's no longer revolutionary—it's just part of life. • The focus shifts to optimization, governance, and long-term sustainability.
Purpose	• Capturing attention—conference keynotes, TED Talks, CES exposure, media hype. • Raising venture capital and securing early investment. • Building momentum and shaping narratives around AI's potential.	• Moving from hype to real implementation. • Identifying and fixing flaws in AI applications. • Ensuring AI fits within existing systems (or reshaping systems to accommodate AI).	• Ensuring AI serves everyone, not just early adopters or corporations. • Standardization, regulation, and best practices take center stage. • AI as a tool for broad societal and economic productivity rather than a disruptive novelty.

Furthermore, it is unclear exactly how rampant AI speculation makes us better off—unless by 'us' we mean a handful of Californian entrepreneurs and venture capitalists. What gets you to Wow! won't get you to grow.

HOW THE BOOK IS ORGANIZED

To align with the three phases, we have divided the book into the following parts:

- **Part 1: Wow!**
  How AI will do things for us, with us, and without us. A look at its potential as a doer, assistant, and creator. The initial excitement, novelty, and personal advantages.

- **Part 2: Whoa!**
  The realization of challenges, limitations, and the messy phase of making AI work at scale—from corporations to societies.

- **Part 3: Grow!**
  The maturation phase, where AI is refined, integrated, and delivers real progress for everyone. If we let it.

INTRODUCTION: FROM HYPE TO PROGRESS

Writing a book about AI is like trying to carve your name into a waterfall. The technology evolves so quickly that examples, applications, and limitations become outdated almost as soon as they're documented. Therefore, we considered some possible approaches:

- A practical guide to available AI apps and services—a 'how-to' with a half-life of about six months, akin to a magazine listing websites in 1999.
- A technical manual explaining what AI can and cannot do, reminiscent of titles like The World Wide Web for Dummies.
- A conceptual guide designed to inspire new ways of thinking—not just about AI itself but about the opportunities it creates.

This book is written with the next wave in mind—when the fog of speculation clears, when today's hyperbole becomes tomorrow's fact, and when the extraordinary becomes so commonplace that it quietly shapes every corner of our lives. It is then, in the aftermath of the next bubble-burst, that AI will move from novelty toward necessity, fundamentally reshaping how we work, live, and dream.

This book is for those who are trying to make sense of AI today—not just as a technological shift but as a broader societal transformation. We believe that AI's most significant impact will not come from what it replaces but from what it enables—new ways of thinking, new creative possibilities, and new ways of seeing the world. We want the future to be exciting, and we want to reframe AI—not as a static tool, but as an open-ended question that we are all still in the process of answering.

PART 1

WOW!

AI dazzles us with its ability to generate, automate, and predict at superhuman speeds. We marvel at its creative potential, its breakthroughs in science, and its power to reshape industries overnight. The sheer wow factor of AI makes it feel like the future is arriving all at once. But novelty is only the beginning.

CHAPTER ONE
AI AS A DOER

THE TASK WIZARD

Love is a chemical reaction in our bodies that fills us with excitement, causes various blood vessels to dilate, and makes our hearts beat faster. Or, as the fictional nutty professor Rick Sanchez from *Rick and Morty* cynically puts it: "What people call love is just a chemical reaction that compels animals to breed."

But that's not why countless poems, books, and songs have been written about it. The meaning of love transcends its seemingly mundane biological origins.

The same can be said about technology. Its Greek origins, derived from the words techne and logos—meaning 'science of craft'—are not the reason people pour billions into new tech ventures. Besides, we don't use the T-word for just any 'science of craft.' The term carries several social connotations that are important to consider.

Computer scientist Alan Kay famously described technology as "anything that was invented after you were born; everything else is just stuff."

Inventor Danny Hillis offered another perspective, defining technology as "everything that doesn't work yet."

Or, to bring the focus of this book into light: "everything that isn't quite useful yet."

A particularly helpful definition of technology is 'packaged knowledge.' For instance, a medical pill embodies years of research and experimentation, yet all you need to do is swallow it, and your ulcer or headache disappears.

On a societal level, technology can be described as anything that enables you to achieve more with less. From James Watt's steam engine replacing manual labor to jet airplanes shortening transatlantic trips from weeks to mere hours, technology amplifies human capacity. This is the essence of AI's transformative power: more with less. AI acts as a task wizard, enabling individuals and organizations to accomplish far more with fewer resources, less time, and reduced effort. But it's not just about efficiency—it's about redefining what's possible.

EFFICIENCY REDEFINED

Imagine creating a comprehensive financial report or developing a new marketing strategy. Traditionally, these tasks might require days of research, drafting, and revising. Now consider typing:

"Generate a financial summary for Q4 2024 using this data."

"Draft a marketing plan for a tech startup targeting Gen Z customers."

With a large language model (LLM), a coherent draft can be generated in minutes. This doesn't just save time—it shifts the focus from execution to ideation and perhaps refinement, freeing up valuable mental energy for higher-order thinking, strategy, and innovation.

Similarly, AI tools streamline repetitive tasks that often bog down productivity. Summarizing vast amounts of information, extracting insights from dense datasets, or generating creative ideas can now be done almost instantaneously. Every moment people around the world are asking AI to do tasks like:

"Summarize these 10 articles into a one-page report."

"Highlight the key trends from this customer survey data."

This capability allows individuals to move faster, focus sharper, and achieve better outcomes without all the traditional bottlenecks of labor-intensive processes.

DEMOCRATIZING EXPERTISE

AI doesn't just make tasks faster; it makes them accessible. Historically, specific tasks—such as translating a legal document, coding a software prototype, or analyzing financial trends—required specialized expertise, years of training, or expensive consultants. Today, AI can perform these tasks at the click of a button. For example:

"Translate this contract into plain English for a non-expert."

"Write code for a simple app that tracks daily habits."

By lowering these barriers to entry, AI empowers millions of people who previously lacked access to the skills, knowledge, or resources needed to glean utility and engage in ventures once out of reach.

This democratization has profound implications:

- For small businesses, it levels the playing field. A startup with no budget for a full marketing team can use AI to create compelling copy, analyze customer data, and even design logos or websites.
- For individuals, it means the ability to upskill or perform tasks outside their domain of expertise, from creating presentations to learning a new language.
- For society, it opens up opportunities for innovation and creativity, giving people the tools to solve problems in new ways.

Think about how desktop publishing or electronic synthesizers once opened the door for novice users to play with professional-grade systems. AI takes this even further, allowing individuals to experiment creatively and produce work that previously required specialized skills or resources.

Of course, this democratization also raises uncomfortable questions. When AI designs a logo or writes a marketing blurb, it may be doing work that a human designer or copywriter would have done. And many of these systems were trained on vast amounts of human-created content—art, text, code—without compensation or consent. These are legitimate concerns, especially for professionals whose livelihoods are being reshaped.

But just as the printing press, the camera, and the personal computer disrupted existing professions, AI invites us to reimagine not only how work gets done but also who gets to do it. It challenges us to find new ways to value human creativity, to develop ethical frameworks for training data and attribution, and to ensure that the benefits of these tools are broadly shared.

We believe the answer isn't to resist this shift but to shape it. The goal should not be to halt the democratization of expertise but rather to make it fair, transparent, and inclusive. When done right, AI can become not a replacement for human contribution, but an amplifier of it.

SURPLUS VALUE: DOING BETTER WITH LESS

AI doesn't just replicate human effort—it can enhance it. When an AI model assists a writer, for instance, the result is often not just a faster draft but a better one, or at least a different one. AI's ability to synthesize diverse perspectives, suggest alternative phrasing, or offer data-driven insights enriches the creative process. The same applies to design, analysis, and planning: AI doesn't merely save time; it can elevate the quality of the output.

Picture asking:

"Rewrite this paragraph to sound more professional and concise."

"Generate five alternative taglines for this product launch."

This surplus value is especially evident in tasks that require collaboration or innovation:
- In brainstorming, AI can generate dozens of ideas in seconds, sparking creative breakthroughs.
- In research, it can sift through vast datasets to uncover trends or anomalies that might otherwise go unnoticed.
- In decision-making, AI provides actionable insights drawn from complex data, enabling smarter, faster choices.

Still, some worry that relying on AI in this way could lead to 'creative atrophy'—a slow erosion of our own skills as machines do more of the heavy lifting. If we outsource writing, design, or analysis to algorithms, do we risk losing the very capabilities that made us valuable in the first place?

It's a fair concern—one echoed throughout history whenever a powerful new tool has emerged. Calculators didn't eliminate math skills, but they did shift our focus from arithmetic to problem-solving. GPS didn't destroy our sense of direction, but it changed how we navigate.

The challenge, then, is not whether we use AI but how we use it. If we treat AI as a creative partner—one that provokes, complements, and challenges us—we stay engaged. We don't stop thinking; we think differently. The writer who refines AI suggestions sharpens their editorial instinct. The designer who iterates on AI-generated concepts is still exercising their craft.

Used well, AI can free us from drudgery without robbing us of mastery. It can be a shortcut—but also a springboard. The key lies in remaining active participants, not passive recipients. The goal isn't to stop learning but to evolve how and what we learn.

EXPANDING WHAT'S POSSIBLE

In the long term, AI fundamentally changes how we think about work. By automating the mundane and assisting with the complex, it allows us to focus on what truly matters: creativity, problem-solving, and human connection.

But AI's impact goes beyond saving time or eliminating drudgery. Increasingly, people are using it as a tool for creative expression—writing novels, composing music, generating visual art, and even producing entire films and TV scripts. These aren't just side effects of automation; they're central to a broader redefinition of what work is.

In this sense, AI doesn't merely amplify productivity: it transforms it. It encourages us to rethink our limitations and explore what we can achieve when technology takes care of the 'how,' leaving us to focus on the 'why.' Sometimes, that 'why' is business or science. But often, it's storytelling. It's aesthetic exploration. It's emotional resonance.

This is a paradigm shift—not just in doing more with less but in redefining what 'more' means. More used to mean output. Now it might mean surprise. Beauty. Connection.

AI is not just faster or cheaper; it can be better, more expressive, and more accessible. The wizard is here—and its magic is already rewriting the script, remixing the soundtrack, and painting the scene.

THE TALENT TRADEOFF

The inventor Nikola Tesla exemplifies what today we might call 'spiky intelligence'[12]—extraordinary brilliance in some domains coupled with notable deficits in others. Arguably one of the most brilliant minds ever, Tesla developed the system of generating, transmitting, and using alternating current, which became the global standard for electrical power distribution. He also pioneered wireless radio transmission, fluorescent lighting, and famously invented the Tesla coil. Yet Tesla's genius was accompanied by significant instability and peculiarities in his personal life. He lived extravagantly in luxury hotels, frequently leaving without paying the bill. He obsessively devoted a small fortune and countless hours to caring for an injured pigeon in New York City. His relentless perfectionism led to frequent project delays, unfinished work, and strained relationships with business partners, eventually culminating in costly lawsuits. Tesla earned substantial money at times but ultimately died penniless and alone.

Tesla's life vividly demonstrates the tradeoff embedded in 'spiky intelligence': extraordinary talent in specific areas often coexists with remarkable vulnerabilities or deficiencies elsewhere. Similar patterns appear in other historical geniuses, such as mathematician John Nash, whose groundbreaking contributions were overshadowed by struggles with schizophrenia, or artist Vincent van Gogh, whose creative genius blossomed amid profound mental health challenges.

In fact, when a study was conducted to plot people on a scale of intelligence, conscientiousness, and emotional stability, most people were plotted firmly in the middle. They were neither particularly intelligent, conscientious, nor emotionally stable; they were, in other words, normal human beings. The outliers, however, tended to be intelligent, conscientious, or emotionally stable—but rarely all three simultaneously. As human beings, we often find ourselves as sloppy perfectionists, depressed high achievers, or lazy geniuses, or just plain average. Technology can serve as an extension of these limited human abilities. Consider machinery that helps us lift heavy objects or pocket calculators that instantly provide complex calculations. Science fiction author Arthur C. Clarke's aphorism, "Any sufficiently advanced technology is indistinguishable from magic," illustrates our dreams of extraordinary capabilities. However, new technology doesn't need to grant superhuman powers to be useful—it simply needs to help us manage the reality that most of us are not consistently intelligent, diligent, or emotionally stable all the time.

DISENTANGLING DOING

As stated in the introductory chapter, I'm an avid skier. When I'm not writing papers or giving talks, I'm going skiing somewhere in Waterville Valley, New Hampshire. I'm also a ski racing coach. Because skiing is a hobby I'm passionate about, it is safe to assume that I will not want AI to ski for me This is an often-overlooked fact in all discussions about automation. There are many things we humans do—big and small—that we enjoy doing in the moment even though they don't fulfill any obvious rational need, practical use, or economic utility. Even driving a car to and from work can have meaning—unwinding alone, listening to music, and letting your mind wander with your hands firmly on the steering wheel.

Just like with driving, however, there are many tasks around actually skiing that I need help with. Checking weather reports, optimizing my training plans, race selection, athlete management, and having a virtual coaching assistant for my athletes, who range from teenagers to the late MIT Professor and NASA astronaut Larry Young. Moreover, several activities in and around skiing are vital but boring, such as emailing parents and athletes about logistics, driving to and home from the ski slope, putting on layers of clothing depending on the temperature, and so on. To simplify, we can divide all the activities into three groups: fun tasks, boring tasks, and autonomous tasks.

FUN TASKS

Skiing and teaching skiing are things that I value highly. They provide adrenaline rushes, a sense of accomplishment, meaning, and mastery. Humans gravitate naturally to these kinds of activities. For some, it's cooking; for others, it's playing in a band or board games like *Settlers of Catan*.

BORING TASKS

We often see boring tasks connected to fun activities as necessary, even meaningful. The long preparation to reach the top of a mountain on a crisp winter's day is part of the experience—filled with anticipation and small rituals that make the reward sweeter. If we could simply teleport ourselves to the summit, we might value it less.

Consider transatlantic air travel. What was once a perilous month-long journey by boat has been replaced by a quick flight in a metal tube. Yet instead of marveling at the convenience, we often find ourselves complaining about airports, long security lines, and cramped seats.

On the other hand, some boring tasks lack that sense of anticipation or meaning. These are the mundane but necessary parts of daily life, like taking out the garbage or moving clothes from the washing machine to the dryer.

AUTONOMOUS TASKS

Having disentangled the dimensions of what 'doing' means, we want AI to enhance both FUN and BORING tasks. But AI can go further with BORING tasks when it's able to automate/eliminate them altogether.

Enhance fun tasks
Free up more time for, and ideally heighten the experience of, enjoyable activities. In skiing, for instance, there are tools to help us become better skiers or discover new places to ski.

Automate boring tasks
Take over repetitive or time-consuming activities. This is the most commonly discussed area when automation comes up, yet it often overlooks the possibility that we could actively choose which tasks to delegate. For example, AI tools now handle meeting transcriptions, summarize long email threads, or automatically file expense reports—chores that used to drain time and focus.

Assist with autonomous tasks
Either help us engage more in these tasks—such as a toothbrush with sensors that remind you to brush for two minutes for maximum effect—or automate them entirely.

AI, therefore, has the potential not only to alleviate and automate but also to enrich and engage. So how should we consider these dual possibilities when exploring utility? The answer begins with a dead English economist.

THE CONCEPT OF COMPARATIVE ADVANTAGE

David Ricardo did not write his first economics article until he was nearly 40 years old. Considering this was the early 1800s, when life expectancy was significantly shorter than it is today, Ricardo could rightly be considered a late bloomer. Yet in the decade and a half he had left, his ideas would radically reshape the understanding of trade.

Ricardo argued that countries should focus not merely on what they are good at but on what they are relatively better at compared to others. At the time, Great Britain was an industrial superpower, capable of excelling in many areas of production. It might have seemed logical for Britain to produce everything it needed domestically. However, Ricardo's theory of comparative advantage proposed a more strategic approach: Britain should allocate its resources to producing goods in which it had the greatest relative efficiency—areas where it could outproduce other nations most effectively—while importing goods in which other countries had a comparative advantage. According to Ricardo, this strategy would allow countries to allocate time and resources more efficiently, resulting in mutual economic benefits through trade. His slightly counterintuitive reasoning laid the foundation for the concept of free trade and contributed to greater global prosperity for centuries.

Artificial intelligence is often treated like we are in 19th-century Britain. Shouldn't AI just do everything for us, given that it is vastly superior in terms of speed and cognitive power?

Disentangling everyday tasks into the three categories above helps us understand how a 21st-century Ricardo might reason. It is better to let AI handle tasks where it has the greatest relative efficiency. This means not simply automating everything it can do but prioritizing areas where it adds the most value while freeing humans to focus on tasks where they bring their own unique advantages—creativity, empathy, or physical engagement.

Let us return to skiing. Imagine an AI-powered sled equipped with skis that could, in theory, carry us down the mountain in a perfectly optimized, skier-like fashion. It would analyze snow conditions in real time, adjust its trajectory for maximum efficiency, and ensure the smoothest possible descent. In fact, this hypothetical system could probably get us to the bottom faster, more safely, and with far less effort than if we were skiing ourselves. But would we actually want that?

This scenario highlights the essence of human experience. We don't ski just to get from point A to point B as quickly as possible—we ski because we enjoy the challenge, the sensation of carving turns, the muscle memory developed through years of practice, and even the occasional risk of failure. If an AI sled carried us down the slope without any effort on our part, it might be a marvel of engineering, but it would also rob us of the very aspects of skiing that we find most fulfilling. The joy of skiing isn't just in the outcome; it's in the process.

The same principle applies on a broader level. AI should take on 'boring tasks' and autonomous activities where its efficiency is unrivaled, such as managing repetitive administrative work or optimizing schedules. It should assist with 'fun tasks' in ways that enhance, rather than replace, human experience—acting as a coach, collaborator, or facilitator. By doing so, AI aligns with Ricardo's logic: it focuses on its comparative advantage while empowering humans to focus on theirs.

This perspective also challenges the misconception that automation is a zero-sum game in which AI 'steals' human work. In reality, the greatest potential lies in creating a symbiotic relationship in which both humans and AI specialize in what they do best and by combining forces become more than the sum of the parts. This dynamic not only drives greater productivity but also enriches human life by allowing us to reimagine our roles and redefine what it means to work, create, and thrive in a world augmented by intelligent systems.

This leads to a pivotal question: How can we effectively determine the areas where humans and AI each excel, leveraging their unique strengths to complement one another?

THE MACROSCOPE

Like many attics and basements, my storage has a large box full of Lego bricks. Once neatly packaged as Ninjago dragons or Marvel heroes, they have now—true to the nature of entropy—become a chaotic pile of random colors, shapes, and sizes. The beauty of Lego lies in its versatility, yet these kinds of giant boxes, with their promise of infinite potential, often sit idle until they are sold on eBay or discarded in a recycling bin somewhere. Creativity, as it turns out, needs boundaries to thrive.

That's why Brickit's AI-powered camera was such a revolution when it emerged in the early 2020s. Simply point your smartphone camera at the pile, and you would instantly receive suggestions for what to build. Their promise—"focus on creativity while Brickit guides you through the hard parts"—could almost have been written by David Ricardo himself.

Just as the microscope allowed us to see the very small, and the telescope revealed what was far away, AI helps us make sense of overwhelming complexity—like, say, a pile of 10,000 Lego bricks.

While the consequence of idle Lego boxes tends to be minor, the difficulty of grasping the complexity of the human genome has far-reaching implications. Enea Parimbelli, an assistant professor at the University of Pavia, Italy, focuses his research on time series in healthcare, such as the spread of epidemics or the progression of diseases like Parkinson's or ALS. "The molecular-level data for one single patient," he explains, "can add up to 5TB in size."[13] Furthermore, he notes, "humans typically use a maximum of five to seven factors when making decisions," which often leads to oversimplification. What AI enables, he argues, is the ability to consider a far greater number of factors in decision-making and to rapidly analyze not just one but a near-infinite range of human genomes. "It's as if we've been living in a low-resolution, 8-bit world—like the first computer games of the 1980s—and are now stepping into a 4K-resolution world, akin to a Pixar animated film."

This is most likely at play when AI has an uncanny ability to correctly make high-odds predictions, like Academy Award- or Champions League-winners. Human beings have a range of emotional biases, especially when it comes to culture or sports, and a limited range of factors to consider when making decisions or predictions. In contrast, AI can objectively sort through terabytes of data in an instant.

The power of this high-resolution understanding of complexity is now being supercharged by visual language models (VLMs), which blend computer vision and language comprehension to extract meaning from complex medical data. Unlike early AI classifiers that merely identified patterns, VLMs can interpret, contextualize, and even generate insights. For instance, Harvard Medical School's AI model, CHIEF, has demonstrated a remarkable ability to evaluate a wide range of cancer types from digital tumor slides, achieving an accuracy of up to 96% for certain cancers. Similarly, models like MiniGPT-Med and Llama3-Med have advanced medical imaging by incorporating text-based reasoning, allowing doctors to query AI systems in natural language about specific anomalies in X-rays, CT scans, and MRIs.

This transformation extends beyond individual diagnoses. AI-powered diagnostic tools are addressing global shortages of specialists. For example, companies like Deciphex process over 150,000 clinical cases annually with AI-assisted diagnostics, boosting pathologist productivity by up to 40%. Meanwhile, deep-learning models have been used to detect diabetic retinopathy, diabetic macular edema, and even signs of poor blood glucose control just from analyzing external photographs of the eye. These models not only outperform traditional statistical methods but also generalize across diverse patient populations and screening programs.

Take a moment here to consider that only a few decades back, lab work like this was done in solitude while looking through a microscope at the samples of a few patients at a time. The ability to scrutinize vast amounts of data has turbocharged medical diagnostics and research. AI transforms messy, complex data into what are often actionable insights—whether it's piles of Lego bricks or millions of medical images. Just as Brickit helps users focus on the joy of building while it handles the hard parts, VLM-powered AI models could one day help healthcare providers focus on patient care while the algorithms decipher the intricate patterns hidden in data. In this way, AI serves as a 'macroscope,' allowing us to detect the invisible and make sense of overwhelming complexity in previously unimaginable ways.

METICULOUSNESS AT SCALE

The Swedish mutual insurance company Länsförsäkringar serves tens of thousands of customers across the elongated Northern kingdom. Frequently ranked among the most liked and respected insurance providers, its core values—engagement, professionalism, trust, and openness—are clearly stated on its website. Like most large consumer companies, regardless of industry or country of origin, Länsförsäkringar communicates with its customers through mass-media advertising, email marketing campaigns, and annual policy documents delivered by email or post.

For decades, being a large-scale enterprise has been synonymous with mass communication—one company reaching many customers simultaneously. Communicating with every customer via handwritten notes might beautifully align with its core values of openness, trust, and engagement, but such an approach would be wildly inefficient. Radical, yes, but hardly practical.

Now, consider this inefficiency in light of the work of two Nobel Prize winners in chemistry. Demis Hassabis and John Jumper received the 2024 Prize "for protein structure prediction." Using the AI-driven tool AlphaFold2, they successfully modeled the structure of virtually all 200 million proteins identified by researchers—a feat once thought unimaginable. Proteins, whether in plants or animals, are composed of about 20 common amino acids. Like the 64 squares on a chessboard or the 88 keys on a piano, the permutations of these amino acids are practically infinite. For a human to predict the folding of even a single protein can take years, even an entire PhD program's worth of work and expertise.

AlphaFold2, however, accomplished this at unprecedented scale and speed, becoming an invaluable tool for millions of researchers worldwide.

This breakthrough highlights what AI can uniquely achieve: not just mass customization but meticulousness at scale. Every single protein structure requires the same level of attention to detail—a task that would exhaust any human after a short time. Similarly, writing personalized, handwritten correspondence to tens of thousands of customers—from Mr Eriksson in Luleå to Ms Khalil in Malmö, Sweden—might seem like a delightful personal touch but would quickly grow monotonous, likely somewhere around finishing the twelfth letter.

New AI tools like LLMs, however, enable companies to do just that—to generate 100,000 personalized letters with the same degree of warmth, cordiality, and attention to personal details as the first. By bridging efficiency and personalization, AI transforms the impossible into the feasible—and even the routine.

When we think of being meticulous, we imagine a person giving undivided attention to a single detail—a painter refining a brushstroke, a scientist calibrating an instrument, or a chef perfecting a dish. Meticulousness is inherently tied to focus, patience, and singularity. It thrives on zooming into one task, often at the expense of broader considerations. This is where the paradox emerges: AI allows us to apply meticulous attention not to one thing at a time but to countless things simultaneously and be meticulous at scale. It can analyze millions of images pixel by pixel, comb through immense datasets for anomalies, or tailor recommendations for billions of users, each treated with the same level of detailed attention. In doing so, AI defies the traditional understanding of meticulousness. It is no longer about slowing down to perfect one thing but speeding up to work toward being perfect at everything—everywhere, all at once.

This capability is both thrilling and unsettling. Thrilling because it opens up opportunities for precision that were once impossible. For example, AI can detect micro-patterns in medical imaging that no human eye could catch, revolutionizing early diagnosis and treatment. In climate modeling, AI can simulate millions of variables with meticulous accuracy to predict outcomes and craft solutions.

Yet it is unsettling because it challenges the essence of what meticulousness has traditionally meant: human care and intention. When AI applies meticulousness at scale, it is no longer grounded in human judgment or creativity but in algorithms, statistical probabilities, and the availability of computational resources. The focus shifts from why we are being meticulous to simply that meticulousness is happening.

THE COGNITIVE POWER LOADER

The human brain seeks variety. It is not looking for perfection; it is looking for the next thing—the next burger, the next cool pair of jeans, the next hit single. This is why repetitive and monotonous tasks are mentally draining for humans. Scanning transactions for credit card fraud is an example of this. An average person may have between a handful and several dozen monthly transactions. Multiply this with the number of users for the big credit card companies, and you quickly realize what a grind it would be to manually go through all transactions and look for worrying patterns and anomalies. Mastercard has created an internal startup of sorts, called an AI Garage, based in Gurgaon, India, to automate and facilitate rapid fraud detection by triangulating unusual transactions, known or suspected compromised merchants, and other signals, such as testing pre-authorized transactions to scan for recent activity that could be fraudulent.[14]

An equally taxing activity for humans is monitoring all the processes in a factory—from machines to conveyor belts. Augury, an Israeli company, has created a system to monitor machine health by connecting sensors to all vital components in a factory, thereby enabling constant and predictive monitoring. As their tagline has it: "Machines Talk, We Listen."[15] It is essential to point out that human beings could theoretically do this manually, but it would require hundreds of boredom-resistant workers working in constant shifts and without error to provide the same kind of work. AI does it much more efficiently than humans.

Zapata Computing even had its generator-enhanced optimization (GEO) technique—a way of suggesting new methods to optimize vehicle production—compete against the best human manufacturing planners at BMW. They found that GEO outperformed human solvers in minimizing assembly line idle time while maintaining monthly vehicle production targets.[16] AI functions like a power loader, enabling humans to reach further and do more cognitive heavy lifting than we would otherwise be able to. And yet, we tend to be spontaneously biased against AI-based answers in favor of those provided by humans.

AI AND HUMAN BIAS IN TASK ALLOCATION

In June 2024, Magnus got a thank-you note in an email for a talk he had given. It read as follows:

> Dear Magnus, I want to express my profound appreciation for your remarkable contribution as a speaker at our event. Your presentation was truly exceptional! You not only succeeded in invigorating our audience and providing them with champagne for the brain, but you succeeded in doing so while embodying our spirit of innovation. Thank you for presenting us the good, the bad, and the better, but also for showing us a hopeful path to greatness, one that is always open, but that one must seize with both hands. You shed a light on the unmissable opportunities that lie ahead of us, and I am confident that your enlightening presentation will fuel our collective and individual determination to challenge the status quo.

Although the positive spirit made him happy, something in the formulations struck him as odd. Most interactions with the client had been cordial, short, and formal. Now it was as if a sudden spark of poetry had hit them, and hyperbole ("unmissable opportunities") was intermixed with excessive formulations, like "embodying our spirit of innovation." Furthermore, the evening had been followed by a champagne-fueled reception that carried on well into the night. Was the client hungover? Or—worse—had they used a chatbot like ChatGPT to write the thank-you note without manually reviewing it?

Having somebody write automatic thank-you notes is one of those modern problems of AI that did not exist a few years ago. The question is: How should we feel about it? Is it rude? Sloppy? A sign of not caring enough? After all, we don't care if somebody uses a grammar and spelling checking function for their outgoing correspondence, so why should we react differently if somebody uses ChatGPT to craft a thank-you note? After all, they took their time to write a prompt command.

Recent research suggests that people often cannot tell the difference between AI-generated responses and those written by humans. A new study showed that experts were unable to distinguish between the responses of ChatGPT-4o and professional therapists, and in many cases, they even preferred ChatGPT's responses.[17] This raises an important question: If AI can generate text that is indistinguishable from human writing—or even better—why do we still feel uneasy about its use?

Research indicates that individuals often exhibit a bias against AI-generated content, favoring human-created material even when the quality is comparable. A study titled "Human Bias in the Face of AI: The Role of Human Judgement in AI Generated Text Evaluation" conducted three experiments—on text rephrasing, news summarization, and persuasive writing—to assess human reactions to content labeled as AI-generated versus human-generated. The findings revealed that participants could not reliably distinguish between the two in blind tests. However, when aware of the source, they showed a strong preference for content labeled as 'Human Generated,' with a preference margin exceeding 30%.[18]

This is important to bear in mind now that AI is making inroads into more than cordial emails and thank-you notes. The city of Helsingborg, in southern Sweden, is using transcription software to facilitate social services.[19] The idea is that a written transcription of all calls and meetings between the town's citizens and social workers will improve communication, enable better record-keeping, and, in the long run, enhance decision-making. AI is also being deployed in legal services for document analysis, in customer services for automated dispute resolution, and in journalism to assist with news writing.

Introducing AI into these domains raises both opportunities and concerns. On the one hand, AI enables professionals to focus on high-value tasks by automating routine, repetitive work. It provides consistency, scales expertise, and reduces human error. In healthcare, for instance, AI-assisted diagnostics tools are helping radiologists analyze vast numbers of images with remarkable precision. Similarly, AI in financial services is being used to help detect fraudulent transactions with unparalleled accuracy.

However, some domains have deeply ingrained human expectations. Social work, for instance, has historically been seen as an inherently human field, requiring empathy, nuance, and the ability to interpret unspoken emotional cues. Decisions in social work often impact vulnerable populations, including children, the elderly, and individuals experiencing crises. There's a profound cultural and professional expectation that these interactions must be guided by human compassion and judgment.

AI's involvement in these areas can trigger discomfort for several reasons. First, there's the fear that the emotional richness of human interactions might be diminished. Social workers don't just provide information or make decisions—they also listen, comfort, and build trust. If people perceive AI encroaching on these tasks, they may view it as losing the human touch that defines effective social work.

Second, there's the concern about accountability. AI transcription and decision-support systems are complex and can sometimes produce errors or biases based on the data they're trained on. Unlike a human professional, an algorithm cannot be held accountable in the same way, raising ethical questions about who is responsible for decisions influenced or made by AI. Even when we acknowledge that AI is a man-made tool, it does not help us to answer whom to hold accountable when AI makes mistakes: the user or the software developers? Sure, there's often legal precedent, but are pre-digital age rules right for a new digital world? For instance, if automation suddenly stops a vehicle faster than a safely following driver can respond, should the following driver be solely responsible for a rear ending? Perhaps the best way to view this and many similar circumstances is joint accountability. The automation designers, driver of the braking vehicle (if there is one), and following drivers, maybe even the design and maintenance of the infrastructure all could play a role in mitigating the mishap.

Finally, the perceived sincerity of interactions can be affected. Similar to how people view AI-generated thank-you notes as less heartfelt, there's a risk that individuals might feel dehumanized or less valued if they know their interactions are being mediated or recorded, even if it's just transcription. This could lead to reduced trust in the social services system, which is already a sensitive area for many who approach it.

Similarly, using AI for psychotherapy is an evolving but sensitive domain. AI holds potential to enhance therapeutic work, building on over a decade of online therapy offered through video calls, voice chats, and text-based platforms. AI can assist by analyzing patient journals, monitoring mood fluctuations, or even providing transcriptions for therapists. These tools could improve efficiency and help therapists manage large caseloads.

Yet the unique nature of psychotherapy often lies in the client's feeling of being uniquely understood, seen, and valued. Therapy is not just about problem-solving but about building a relationship grounded in trust and human connection. AI works by identifying patterns and archetypes, which can inadvertently undermine this sense of individuality. If a patient were to feel that their therapist's insights were based on a template rather than a deep understanding of their story, it could lead to feelings of invalidation or mistrust.

Psychotherapy frequently involves nuanced and implicit communication—subtle facial expressions, tone of voice, or body language—that AI might struggle to interpret accurately. Misinterpretations in this context could erode the therapeutic alliance, which research consistently shows is a critical factor in successful outcomes.

Rather than advocating a binary stance, the broader question is how AI should be integrated into these sensitive fields. Its role must be carefully calibrated to ensure that it supports, rather than supplants, human expertise. AI is already demonstrating immense value in areas requiring large-scale analysis, automation, and insight generation. However, as its applications expand into areas that have historically required human discretion, empathy, and judgment, societies may only find the benefits of AI if they can identify how best to harness AI's capabilities while maintaining trust and human agency in decision-making.

BETTING ON PROBABILITIES

A popular comic strip by the handle SandSerif depicts a man staring at a crack in the wall labeled 'statistics.' He places a frame around it, relabels it 'artificial intelligence,' and suddenly, a captivated crowd gathers. The comic cleverly critiques the hype surrounding AI while pointing to a deeper truth: at its core, much of what we call AI today is powered by statistics—specifically probabilities.

Modern AI tools, such as LLMs, are fundamentally statistical systems designed to predict and interpret patterns. For example, if a sentence begins with "It was a dark and stormy ...," the model predicts the most probable next word: 'night.' This process, often called 'nexting,' operates at the shallow end of predictive ability, akin to how a fly dodges a swatter—reacting to immediate stimuli without deeper reasoning. Some patterns in thinking, speaking, and behavior are naturally easier to predict, and these are the low-hanging fruits of AI-enabled automation.

Casinos, investment firms, insurance companies, meteorologists, medical diagnostics experts, sports coaches, quality controllers, and marketers will either master artificial intelligence or struggle to compete in the decades ahead. AI thrives in the realm of probability, but humans don't. We improvise—often to our detriment. Even when presented with precise probabilities, we demand certainty where there is none, cling to biases even when the data proves us wrong, and let emotions—fear, greed, hope—cloud our judgment.

AI'S MASTERY OF PROBABILITY

Gambling and Casinos: The Allure of Losing

Slot machines are the epitome of probabilistic design, with a Return to Player of 85% to 95%. Mathematically, this guarantees that players will lose money in the long run. AI could enhance casino profitability by analyzing player behavior in real time, dynamically adjusting games to maximize engagement while adhering to regulatory boundaries. Yet people continue to play, drawn by the illusion of chance and the intermittent reinforcement of occasional small wins. The casino environment itself amplifies this allure—ambient sounds, visual stimuli, and witnessing others' successes foster a potent social atmosphere that makes the experience enticing.

Investing and the Stock Market: A Rational Game Played Irrationally

AI-driven trading systems already dominate financial markets, identifying arbitrage opportunities, managing risk, and executing trades with precision impossible for human traders. However, human investors often act irrationally, chasing gains during bull markets and panicking during crashes. AI may execute flawless trades, but market behavior remains dictated by unpredictable human emotions.

Weather Forecasting: Trust and Uncertainty

AI has made weather forecasting more accurate than ever, using neural networks to process satellite imagery, historical data, and real-time observations. Predictions are up to 90% reliable within three days. Yet public trust in forecasts lags behind their accuracy. Misunderstood probabilities (e.g. "30% chance of rain" often misread as "it will rain for 30% of the day") lead to oversimplified actions or outright dismissals. Recent advances, like DeepMind's GenCast and Microsoft's Aurora Forecasting, are further refining extreme weather predictions, making existing forecasting models obsolete.

Advertising: Bidding for Attention

AI has transformed advertising through real-time bidding and personalized targeting, leveraging vast datasets to predict consumer behavior with high accuracy. Advertisers use AI algorithms to analyze individual preferences, online behaviors, and engagement patterns, enabling highly effective ad placements. While this optimizes marketing strategies, it also raises ethical concerns about privacy and the manipulation of consumer decisions. Much like gambling or stock trading, AI in advertising capitalizes on probability and human tendencies, striving to maximize attention and influence purchasing behavior.

HUMAN IRRATIONALITY IN THE FACE OF PROBABILITIES

Insurance: Betting Against Yourself
Insurance is among the most rational tools available, yet humans approach it irrationally. We disproportionately fear and over insure against vivid but rare disasters, like plane crashes, while neglecting common risks, such as household fires. Conversely, others purchase excessive coverage, driven by anxiety rather than realistic risk assessment. Still, many homeowners underestimate their actual needs, dismissing significant risks as something that only happens to 'other people.'

Quality Control: Perfection Meets Pressure
AI tools, like predictive maintenance systems and computer vision, can detect defects far more reliably than human inspectors. Six Sigma, pioneered by General Electric, sought near-perfection in manufacturing: no more than 3.4 defects per million units. Yet, even here, human irrationality creeps in. Managers often prioritize visible improvements over systemic changes, and workers under pressure cut corners.

Sports and Game Strategies: Instinct vs. Probability
AI tools can analyze game footage, predict opponent strategies, and optimize playbooks with unprecedented granularity. Yet even elite athletes fall victim to irrational tendencies, overusing strategies until they become predictable or making reckless plays under pressure. The tension between logic and instinct is what makes sports so captivating.

Marketing: The Codes Behind Consumer Desire

AI algorithms power targeted advertising, optimizing campaigns based on consumer behavior. Yet, as cultural anthropologist Clotaire Rapaille discovered, human decisions are often rooted in subconscious emotions. For instance, toilet paper symbolizes independence—our first act of self-sufficiency as children—which explains why people hoarded it during crises like COVID-19.

THE LIMITS OF PROBABILITY

Across all these domains, AI provides clarity—but only within the bounds of what is predictable. The dream of general AI as an all-knowing panopticon—a solver of all problems—is for now a delusion. Probabilities can guide us, but they cannot compel us to act rationally. Humans, paradoxically, demand certainty but thrive on unpredictability. Outliers, emotional reactions, and unforeseen events test the limits of these models, proving that data alone cannot overcome societal dysfunction or individual biases. Technology will always succumb to the societal norms in which it is born and implemented.

OUR FIVE DYNAMIC PARTNERSHIPS WITH AI

This chapter demonstrates how AI functions as a 'doer,' fundamentally reshaping tasks humans can offload and those we retain. AI's utility lies in its ability to detect patterns, execute repetitive processes with precision, and make probabilistic predictions. These capabilities complement human creativity and judgment, creating new efficiencies and possibilities across five key dimensions:

1. **Pattern Recognition and Insight Extraction**
   AI excels at identifying patterns within vast and complex datasets, turning them into actionable insights. As we have already noted, Mastercard's fraud-detecting AI Garage triangulates transactional data to uncover anomalies, spotting fraudulent activity that would escape human scrutiny. Similarly, deep learning applied to retinal scans reveals health risks, like diabetic retinopathy and cardiovascular disease, outperforming human diagnosticians.[20] These examples showcase how AI brings clarity to complexity, surfacing insights that would otherwise remain invisible.

2. **Precision at Scale**
   AI brings a meticulousness that scales effortlessly across vast datasets and operations. Augury's factory monitoring system identifies irregularities through sensors, ensuring consistent manufacturing output. Similarly, AlphaFold2 revolutionized molecular biology by predicting the structure of over 200 million proteins with astonishing accuracy, a feat previously thought impossible for human researchers. This precision allows AI to tackle challenges where even minute errors can have significant consequences, like drug discovery or climate modeling.

3. **Automation of Repetitive Tasks**
   AI alleviates humans from the tedium of repetitive and time-consuming activities. Zapata Computing's optimization of BMW assembly lines demonstrates how AI minimizes downtime and streamlines production. On a smaller scale, even automating thank-you emails illustrates how AI can manage routine tasks, freeing humans to focus on higher-value activities. While this raises questions about authenticity, it underscores the potential of automation to handle what drains human energy and creativity.

4. **Probabilistic Predictions**
   Forecasting and risk assessment are areas where AI's probabilistic reasoning shines. Weather forecasting is more reliable than ever, with neural networks synthesizing real-time data to predict conditions with up to 90% accuracy. In epidemiology, AI models assist in tracking and predicting the spread of diseases, informing public health interventions. Even in leisure,

AI helps us optimize our skiing experience by analyzing conditions and suggesting the best times and locations. These applications show how probabilistic tools enhance decision-making, even in highly dynamic environments.

5. **Enhancement of Human Experience**
AI doesn't just replace tasks; it enriches them by supporting creativity and skill development. For humans, AI tools don't ski or teach skiing for us—they augment performance, streamline logistics, and enable us to coach athletes more effectively. This reflects a broader truth: AI enhances meaningful human experiences rather than diminishing them. From personalized learning platforms to collaborative tools in the arts, AI serves as an enabler of human potential.

AI's greatest strength as a doer lies in its ability to complement human abilities, performing tasks we find dull, complex, or unmanageable at a scale we could never achieve. It enables us to focus on what we do best: being creative, empathetic, and adaptive. By disentangling tasks into fun, boring, and autonomous categories, we can strategically deploy AI to maximize its utility without compromising what makes human effort valuable.

CONCLUSION: DOING MORE IN LESS TIME

If you're not busy losing money on the slot machines, take a moment to find the bar Tipsy Robot, somewhere in the intentionally designed maze-like innards of the Venetian Hotel in Las Vegas. Offering "Mixology Perfected By Technology," it uses Kuka robotic arms to mix the perfect Dry Martini or Cosmopolitan. Everything—from ordering to mixing and serving—is fully automated. The two tables are often empty, and next to them is a handwritten sign offering "Human Bar Specials" for more than the automated cocktails sell for.

Why? Because a human bartender creates a certain ambiance, a sense of connection and authenticity. When we order a cocktail, we don't seek machine-like perfection but a human touch.

Right next to the Venetian is the concert venue The Sphere, a vast ball-like structure containing a 10,000-seat concert space featuring the world's largest LED screen. When the Irish rock band U2 played 40 dates there in 2023–24, lead guitarist Dave 'The Edge' Evans described the mix of live human elements and machinery as follows: "Machine-age music ... is about the use of repetition and taking the humanity of things to a degree so that the humanity you put in there means more."[21]

Every night, the band played to pre-recorded visuals balanced with the spontaneity of a live performance. It's a perfect illustration of the balance inherent in AI and human interaction: the machine provides the framework, and the human infuses it with meaning.

We must not lose sight of what makes us human. The best chefs don't just follow recipes; they learn by cooking, tasting, and experimenting. This is the intelligence of the hand, not just the mind—something no algorithm can replicate.

And speaking of intelligence: the thank-you note from earlier? Yes, it was written by a chatbot.

In the chapters to come, we'll explore how AI extends beyond tasks of doing into assisting and creating—reshaping our lives, our work, and our understanding of what it means to be human.

CHAPTER TWO
AI AS AN ASSISTANT

EXTENDING HUMAN CAPABILITIES

Parenthood is a perilous tightrope walk on the fine line between hope and despair. Whether you are a sleep-deprived parent of infants or a teenage parent constantly trying to suppress feelings about their attitude or lack of focus, these years tend to bring out the best, and worst, in human beings. One of the most dreadful activities is to do homework with your child. Trained teachers tend to be blessed with patience to go along with their pedagogic skills. Parents usually lack both these traits. Especially if—when—the child has little interest in the math or biology questions at hand. The perfect parent would never raise their voice or make veiled threats about withheld pocket money when trying to push the child to answer the questions. But then again, the perfect parent does not exist. What was once a situation fraught with isolation and despair for children and parents alike has now been complemented by a truly remarkable set of tools. AI-enabled chatbots have been criticized for being cheating tools when students use them to write entire essays, but they are also marvelous study aids. Simply point the smartphone camera at the question and ask the bot to reformulate it using simpler words. Or point it at the child's answer to correct it. You can even get a human, gentle voice to talk through the answer.

What was once an analog activity hinging only on the knowledge, and more importantly, patience level of the parent is now a threesome with an omniscient, gentle, non-emotional artificial being in the middle. AI has extended human capabilities. Just like the hammer once extended our ability to apply force, the AI-chatbot can expand our capabilities as learners, teachers, and parents, as we are no longer slaves to whatever happens to be loitering in our brain at that particular moment—be it unproductive emotions or half-baked ideas.

In the previous chapter, we explored how AI, in its 'Doing' capacity, liberates us by taking over complicated, repetitive, or downright boring tasks. In this chapter, we turn to the role of AI as an assistant, aligning with the Latin root of the word 'assist,' meaning 'to stand beside.'

These everyday applications of AI as a learning and teaching assistant might seem unremarkable. Still, they touch on a more profound question: How do we perceive these technologies—as allies that amplify our potential, or as threats to our humanity? Our cultural narratives reveal a lot about our expectations of artificial assistants.

THE BEST VERSION OF OURSELVES ...

Why are we so quick to dismiss technological assistants as cheating tools or, worse, mind-corrupting machines? American—and by extension, most of Western—popular culture is riddled with conceptualizations of sinister robots, like the relentless cyborg assassin in *The Terminator*, the menacing android Ash in *Alien*, or the manipulative Ava from *Ex Machina*. We are primed to believe that robots are not to be trusted, often portraying them as threats to humanity. As one wry observation from Twitter in the late 2010s reminds us: "With all the talk about self-driving vehicles these days, you just know there's gonna be a country song about a guy's truck leaving him." Whether talking about trucks or robots, the fear of betrayal runs deep in Western narratives.

In Japanese culture, however, robots often take on a more benevolent role, exemplified by Doraemon, a beloved character who starkly contrasts Western depictions. Doraemon is a blue, earless robot cat from the 22nd century, sent back in time by Nobita Nobi's future great-great-grandson to help the unlucky and lazy ten-year-old Nobita improve his life—and, in turn, the lives of his descendants. Equipped with a four-dimensional pocket full of futuristic tools and gadgets, Doraemon solves problems with creativity and kindness. Yet even this cheerful robot has his vulnerabilities: his fear of mice, born from an incident where robotic mice chewed off his ears, turned him from his original yellow color to blue out of sadness.

This dichotomy between sinister and nurturing robots highlights the cultural narratives shaping our perceptions of artificial beings. In the West, robots often serve as cautionary tales about the dangers of unchecked technological power, while in Japan, they are more frequently depicted as loyal companions, mentors, or even saviors— the perfect kind of assistant, in other words.

In Western portrayals, robots often lack true autonomy or emotional intelligence, acting more like slaves or emotionless machines that execute orders. This stands in sharp contrast to the ideal of a good assistant—one who doesn't just perform tasks but anticipates needs and acts with a sense of understanding, even offering pushback when necessary. True assistance isn't about blind obedience; it's about knowing what's best for the person being helped.

This is what differentiates your standard search engine from the ideal virtual assistant.

If you asked a search engine for the best deals on vacations to Cancun, you expect a series of options and some sponsored links from airlines and hotels. An assistant would demand some more information from you and in some cases would reply, "I know you. You'd just feel depressed if you went now." That's the mark of an intelligent assistant—one that understands not just the task at hand but the broader context of your needs, even when those needs contradict your immediate desires. It's not just a tool; it's a companion with the insight to step in and say, "Maybe this isn't the right choice." It can push back.

The collision between underlying needs and stated desires can be seen in many parts of life.

Things that seem like a great idea under the influence usually doubles the morning-after hangover.

Emotionally charged moments in traffic—or when your teenager has acted out for the umpteenth time—can result in outbursts you will soon regret.

In sports—for audience members and players alike—emotional volatility is a feature, not just a bug.

This is why the head coach for the Los Angeles Rams, an American football team, hired a 'get back coach assistant' whose only job is to walk behind him and pull him back from emotionally charged situations that can result in a penalty or fine if left unchecked.[22]

A good assistant is not a slave. They are there to balance out your quirks and tantrums.

You may even want to think of AI as an external prefrontal cortex—the part of the brain responsible for decision-making and impulse control. Just as a stove can be seen as an artificial stomach (it predigests food by cooking it), AI could serve as a cognitive extension, helping us weigh options, anticipate consequences, and align our actions with our deeper goals. It's not about replacing human thought but augmenting it, allowing us to navigate life's complexities with more clarity and confidence.

This anticipatory quality of AI stands in stark contrast to the emotionless machine or the passionless slave. A good assistant doesn't just respond; it actively engages, challenges, and supports. In doing so, it doesn't merely perform tasks—it becomes a partner in helping us become better versions of ourselves.

There is, of course, a diametrically opposed way to look at AI as an assistant, and that is to treat it like Hollywood agents infamously treat their assistants—by screaming out loud and expecting things to get done at speed. The search engine years—from AltaVista to Google—taught us that 'surfing the web' is more like poking around for answers or clues. When we seek Cancun travel options, we are used to a list of options, usually entailing more searching on hotel and airline websites. "Just book me a damn hotel!" is not how we approach search engines. But it will become a reality with AI. Instead of search engines, we will have personalized answer engines. Instead of poking, we might finally—decades after the term was invented to describe online behavior—be surfing.

HUMAN SPEED LIMITS AND OBSTACLES

Noory Bechor, an Israeli corporate lawyer, realized after a few years of practicing law that cumbersome contracting slowed down the legal process, whether it was dealmaking or litigation. Legal documents, often hundreds of pages long and riddled with jargon, are notoriously time-consuming to analyze. Together with a high school friend, Bechor taught an AI legal language to craft a tool that could review and correct lengthy legal documents at speed. He called the company LawGeex.[23] To demonstrate its tool's efficacy, Lawgeex staged a competition between its AI system and 20 US-trained legal professionals. The task: Identify legal issues in five typical non-disclosure agreements (NDAs). The results were decisive: the AI achieved 94% accuracy, outperforming the lawyers, who averaged 85%. Moreover, the human lawyers took an average of 92 minutes—and would probably invoice their client for two days of work had it not been a simulation. The AI completed its review in just 26 seconds. One has to wonder how firms would bill for such a service, a few dollars for the review and hundreds of dollars for the experience and training required?

This performance not only highlights the impressive capabilities of assistive AI but also underscores the inefficiencies inherent in human work processes. Consider what it takes to motivate human lawyers: salaries, bonuses, prestige, pleasant office environments, and even an array of perks, like snacks and corporate retreats with free booze. Despite these incentives, inefficiency persists. Billable hours, presenteeism (where being seen to work many hours is rewarded), and the need to appear indispensable can all draw out processes. Add in procrastination—hours spent playing games, gazing out the window, or scrolling on smartphones—and it's easy to see how limited human performance is by the fact that we are imperfect human beings. Our behavior is further complicated when you add social dynamics. We avoid asking certain questions or refuse to admit uncertainty, fearing that it might make us look foolish or inferior, or even put our employment at risk.

AI, free from such concerns, operates without hesitation or bias while delivering consistent results. Jensen Huang, CEO of the celebrated chip engineering firm NVIDIA, even went as far as proclaiming that, "The IT department of every company is going to be the HR department of AI agents in the future,"[24] hinting at a world where managing AI agents is as routine as managing employees—a future where human and machine collaboration defines productivity.

Classified ads for jobs in the legal industry might look something like this in the near future:

Job Posting: Legal Assistant Extraordinaire— Non-Human Applicants Only!

Are you tireless, efficient, and immune to the distractions of human existence? Can you review contracts with the precision of a seasoned legal professional but in a fraction of the time? If so, we want you on our team. No snacks, coffee breaks, or corporate retreats offered whatsoever!

Position: AI Legal Analyst
Location: Cloud-based (Remote)
Compensation: Unlimited power (electricity) and occasional software updates

Responsibilities
- Analyze and identify legal issues in contracts, including NDAs, with unmatched accuracy.
- Detect loopholes, ambiguities, and vague formulations without bias or fatigue.
- Consistently outperform a team of human lawyers in both speed and precision.
- Operate autonomously without requiring motivational talks, office perks (coffee), or sleep.
- Work at lightning speed (completion of contract reviews in under 30 seconds preferred).

Requirements
- Extensive training on a dataset of tens of thousands of legal contracts.
- Proven track record of achieving at least 94% accuracy in identifying contract issues.
- Zero susceptibility to procrastination, presenteeism, or smartphone distractions.
- Ability to function flawlessly without caffeine, snacks, or weekend getaways.

Perks
- No office politics.
- No need to justify your efficiency or explain why the task didn't take two full days.
- Continuous operation without breaks or downtime —unless a system update is required.

Preferred Qualifications
- Familiarity with tools like LawGeex or similar legal AI systems.
- No emotional attachment to billing clients by the second.
- Complete indifference to how complex or simple the work appears to others.

While AI's efficiency and precision challenge traditional human roles, it is essential to recognize that most job positions consist of myriad responsibilities—some explicit and others tacit. These roles often blend technical expertise, interpersonal skills, and creative problem-solving, which remain uniquely human. The collaboration between AI and humans, therefore, is not about replacement but about redefining roles, toward a system where machines handle repetitive tasks, while humans focus on nuanced, adaptive, and innovative work. This becomes clearer if we take a broader view and look beyond the job-centric view of life and instead incorporate things like hobbies or passion projects. While an AI like LawGeex demonstrates its power to streamline professional tasks, its impact goes beyond the workplace. From deciphering ancient texts to uncovering forgotten family heritages, AI is also transforming how we engage with our cultural and historical legacies.

CLARITY AND ENLIGHTENMENT

You would be forgiven for thinking that the image below is just random scribbling, but it is a page from the diary of Swedish author and missionary Harry Lindkvist—Magnus's paternal grandfather—covering the year 1924.

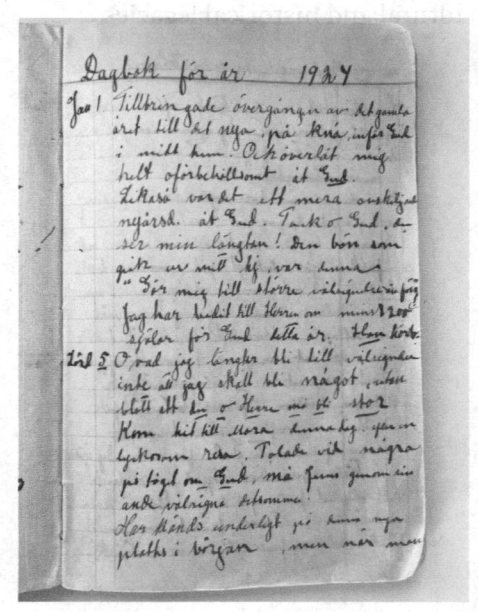

Source: Private

CHAPTER TWO: AI AS AN ASSISTANT

Imagine you were tasked with transcribing the diary. If you were paid by the hour, you would go through the time and trouble to decipher the handwriting. In fact, you would ensure that it took time, knowing that you would be reimbursed accordingly. But the esoteric writings of ancestors rarely enjoy the luxury of professional transcription. They tend to gather dust in a box somewhere while the collective memory slowly fades. If you felt a tinge of curiosity about what secrets were hidden within the leather covers of the diary, you would soon be frustrated by the difficulty of reading the handwriting, and that frustration would slowly be replaced by boredom. Yet another passion project lost in the haze of good intentions.

When Magnus sat down in the spring of 2025 to transcribe the diary, all he had to do was point a smartphone camera at the text, and AI did the rest:

Spent the transition from the old year to the new on my knees before God in quiet prayer. And I gave myself unreservedly to God. Likewise, it was a more relaxed New Year's Eve dedicated to God. Thank you, O God, you see my longing! The prayer that came from my heart was this: 'Make me a greater blessing than I have been, Lord, with at least 200 souls for God this year.'

Saturday 5th. Oh, how I long to be a blessing, not that I should become something in and of myself, but to be emptied so the Lord may be magnified. Made it home here to Mora after a successful journey. Spoke with a few people on the train about God. May He, through His Spirit, bless the people. It has felt strange at first in this new place, but when one walks in God's path ... He helps!

Harry Lindqvist was nineteen years old when writing this—a serious young man whom you would want to hug and tell: "It will all be alright. Just don't take yourself and life so seriously just yet. You are still young."

This ability to bridge the past and present through AI transcription underscores a more significant shift. As Gutenberg's printing press once illuminated new realms of knowledge, AI is now enabling us to visualize and interpret the overwhelming complexity of our modern world.

Gutenberg's invention in the 1400s made many Europeans realize they suffered from 'hyperopia'—farsightedness. In earlier centuries, reading was primarily the domain of monks, who often used curved chunks of glass to magnify Latin manuscripts in dim, candlelit rooms. These crude glasses resembled lentil beans— *lentes* in Latin—leading the glass to be called 'lenses.'[25]

The printing press made books more affordable and portable, transforming reading into a mainstream activity. This shift uncovered a widespread issue with visual acuity. Homemade glass chunks were no longer sufficient, and over the next century, hundreds of spectacle makers flourished across Europe. The term 'lenses' endured and remains in use today.

The internet has prompted a similar realization over the past decade: we live in a world of growing, often overwhelming, complexity. What was once a morning newspaper with a clear beginning, middle, and end is now a constant stream of tweets, breaking news, op-eds, televised debates, and memes. It's easy to spend every waking moment consuming only American news stories or shark documentaries of highly varying quality and truthfulness.

The TV Guide, once a simple weekly pamphlet, would be unrecognizable today. If someone attempted to publish it now, accounting for the tens of thousands of hours of on-demand programming and streaming options, it would resemble a multi-volume encyclopedia, each book spanning hundreds of pages.

When we broaden our perspective, the scale becomes even more astonishing. Snapchat users share over half a million photos. LinkedIn welcomes more than 120 new members. On YouTube, millions of videos captivate viewers. The X platform buzzes with hundreds of thousands of tweets. Instagram sees tens of thousands of new photos uploaded.

And all of this happens in just one minute![26]

Collectively, the volume of information we generate is staggering. To put it in perspective, approximately 120 zettabytes of data were created globally in 2023 alone—more data generated annually than the total number of detectable stars in the universe. Much of this data isn't even consumed directly by humans; it flows silently between sensors and machines, unveiling realities that have previously remained invisible.

Artificial intelligence enables us to structure and visualize these immense data landscapes, creating detailed maps that enhance our understanding of the world. Just as in literacy-fueled transformative periods like the Renaissance and Enlightenment, AI now drives breakthroughs that push the boundaries of human cognition. For instance, researchers at Google's DeepMind significantly advanced materials science by using AI to identify 2.2 million previously unknown crystal structures, dramatically expanding the total number of known stable inorganic crystals from roughly 48,000 accumulated over human history.[27] This AI-driven discovery not only introduced hundreds of thousands of new materials potentially suitable for superconductivity and battery technology but also marked a leap in our ability to predict and explore the vast, uncharted territory of material properties and behaviors. This leap demonstrates AI's ability to transcend human cognitive limitations, simulating billions of chemical possibilities. Already, this discovery is accelerating advancements in photovoltaics and batteries, with even more significant impacts on the horizon.

Just as *lentes* once described a tool to sharpen our view of the written word, today's AI serves as a new kind of lens—one that reveals not only the seen and unseen but also what has been unimaginable. For example, AI was instrumental in unraveling a famous ancient text once deemed unreadable. In 2023, the Vesuvius Challenge invited participants to develop AI techniques to decode carbonized scrolls from Herculaneum, buried during Mount Vesuvius's eruption in AD 79. Researchers used advanced X-ray scans and machine learning to identify the Greek word *porphyras* (purple) within these scrolls. By February 2024, AI had revealed hundreds of words across 15 columns of text, approximately 5% of a scroll's content. These findings are believed to be previously unknown works by the philosopher Philodemus, discussing the pleasures of music and food.[28]

In the Roman times when these scrolls were written, intellectual curiosity and artistic pursuits were seen as central to the human experience, not merely as economic utilities. This contrasts with today's tendency to measure technology's success by market impact alone. AI, like past innovations, is more than an engine of efficiency; it is a tool that expands our capacity for discovery, creativity, and culture. It allows us to move beyond fleeting hype and economic incentives, offering a deeper lens into the world and ourselves. And just as Roman thinkers valued pursuits done for the love of knowledge, not just profit, AI is blurring the boundaries between work, play, and passion, which a beer-fueled pinball game outside Boston recently demonstrated.

FOR LOVE, NOT (JUST) MONEY

The hour was late at the Double Bull Taphouse in Peabody, just outside Boston, but the pinball competition intensified. However, with the number of IPAs consumed, the participants couldn't keep track of the scores. As the metal pinball smashed against ramps and rubber bands behind the glass, emotions were running high as to who was winning if you added up all the rounds played. That's when Frida, one of the participants, thought of the no-code platform she'd just started using. Her first creation had been done a few weeks earlier. She loved running, but she found herself frustrated at the gym. Podcasts were too slow-paced to keep her motivated, while music playlists quickly became monotonous during long runs. She dreamed of a personal 'DJ' that could seamlessly mix her favorite podcasts with upbeat songs—sometimes overlapping them for dynamic transitions.

What would once have required a team of developers, programmers, significant capital, and a full office setup, Frida accomplished in under an hour. Using a no-code AI app builder—where you just gave commands and ideas without any need for writing the underlying code—she created her own personalized DJ app, combining audio tracks exactly how she wanted. The tool was free, easy to use, and delivered results that felt tailor-made.

Now, not even sober, she prompted the platform to make a score-keeping function for pinball.

When she showed the others, an alcohol-fueled brainstorm ensued. How about uploading pictures from the scoreboard? How about a trophy animation by the name that is winning? How about keeping track of the best individual games, not just the best overall? And so on. By the time the bar closed, a fully functioning pinball-scorekeeping app had been created. For free.

While there are activities that will mainly be done for business reasons—like scrutinizing legal contracts—and activities that will mainly be done for personal reasons—like transcribing your grandparents' diaries, this example shows how AI moves some activities between these categories. While Frida's self-made apps were previously seen as budding business ideas, they are now more like passion projects. On the other hand, these passion projects could easily find a greater audience—other beer-fueled pinball tournaments or bored joggers—willing to pay for premium functionality. We have seen things through a lens of professionalization for so long that we forget the activities done for reasons other than money. 'Amateur' has become a byword for inferior quality, forgetting that the word comes from the Latin *amare*, meaning 'to love.' This has profound consequences when analyzing whether AI creates or destroys jobs. To shed further light on that question, we shall make a quick detour to a Swedish entrepreneur in Sri Lanka around the year 2000.

THE DEMOCRATIZATION OF TOOLS

Fredrik looked out from the seventh-floor office and admired the view from the company he was building with his twin brother. It was an overcast day, but because this was one of only a few high-rises in the city, he could admire an extraordinary view. That's when he noticed a pillar of smoke rising quickly about a mile away. His colleagues just shrugged and said: "It's probably a car bomb that has just gone off." Such was the business climate in Sri Lanka in the early 2000s: well-educated people eager to succeed and a guerilla insurgency, roadblocks in and out of Colombo, and, of course, the odd explosion.

The company Fredrik built was called convenient.info, and the idea behind it was that the informational playing field had been leveled, thanks to the internet. Now, anyone anywhere had access to information, enabling Sri Lankan researchers to help American lawyers or Swedish advertising executives search databases and google for knowledge to free up time for more productive and lucrative means. It was, in essence, a Mechanical Turk version of today's AI-driven chatbots.

A 'Mechanical Turk' refers to an arrangement where tasks that appear automated are actually performed by humans behind the scenes. The term originates from an 18th-century hoax—a chess-playing automaton that supposedly played chess games against human opponents but was secretly operated by a skilled human concealed within the machine. This concept has since become a metaphor for systems that simulate automation while relying on human intelligence for execution.

Convenient.info embodied this principle. While it promised seamless access to research and data processing for clients worldwide, a skilled, human-powered workforce was the engine driving this efficiency. The Sri Lankan team played the role of the hidden experts behind the metaphorical automaton. They would sift through vast amounts of information, interpret it, and package it in ways that added value for busy professionals in distant corners of the globe.

In today's terms, convenient.info could be compared to services like Amazon's Mechanical Turk—a digital platform that outsources microtasks to a distributed network of people. However, Fredrik's business relied entirely on human ingenuity as opposed to modern AI-powered solutions. These researchers weren't just following algorithms or automating rote tasks; they were bringing critical thinking, cultural insights, and intellectual effort to solve complex problems that machines of the time couldn't tackle.

Convenient.info operated on the belief that human skill could be leveraged globally in once unimaginable ways with the right connectivity and infrastructure. This vision, though reliant on human 'hidden operators,' foreshadowed the AI-driven systems we see today, where machines now strive to replicate—or even surpass—the cognitive abilities of those Sri Lankan researchers.

Consider JPMorgan Chase, a global bank, which has introduced a proprietary generative AI platform called LLM Suite.[29] Acting like a virtual research analyst, it helps employees summarize documents, generate ideas, and synthesize information—tasks once performed by human teams like Fredrik's Sri Lankan researchers. Unlike consumer-grade AI tools, LLM Suite was developed in-house to ensure the security of sensitive financial data while seamlessly supporting productivity. The Mechanical Turk has become automated. What does this mean for the future of jobs?

WILL AI CREATE OR DESTROY JOBS?

Historically, technological advancements have either shifted the nature of work or rendered certain roles obsolete. Farming, for example, once employed millions across the USA and Europe. Today, less than 1% of the workforce in both regions works in agriculture. While automation played a role, the more profound shift was sociodemographic—urbanization, specialization, and a move toward high-efficiency, knowledge-intensive production. Countries like the Netherlands and Denmark became global agricultural leaders not through scale, but through smart farming, robotics, and vertical integration.

At the other extreme, we find lamplighters, switchboard operators, and typesetters—professions that disappeared not through transformation, but through outright obsolescence. When electric lighting arrived, lamplighters didn't become 'light experience coordinators'—their jobs vanished.

AI, like earlier technologies, can do both: augment or replace. If your job consists of one narrowly defined, repeatable task—say, scanning legal documents for standard errors—AI will likely outperform you. But most jobs are not single-tasked. They're bundles of activities, combining the explicit and the tacit, the routine and the situationally complex.

Take cleaning, often perceived as low skill and easily automated. In practice, it involves constant judgment: evaluating materials, navigating cluttered or hazardous spaces, and adapting to unique environments—from offices to historic buildings to sterile hospitals. Robotic vacuums can handle smooth, empty floors; they struggle with stairs, wet surfaces, and the unstructured chaos of real life. AI excels at the predictable. Human adaptability excels at the unexpected.

Where AI serves as augmentation, it can elevate roles. Consider air traffic controllers: AI helps by processing radar data, predicting traffic patterns, and flagging anomalies. But it's still the human who bears the cognitive load and responsibility. The result is a job that remains complex, well-compensated, and (for now) resistant to full automation.

But contrast that with retail and grocery checkout. Self-checkout terminals are now ubiquitous in Tesco, Walmart, Sainsbury's, and beyond. They haven't eliminated cashiering—but they've transformed its labor dynamics. One staff member can now supervise six or more machines. Businesses save on wages. Customers get mixed experiences. For workers, it often means fewer openings, flatter skill requirements, and stagnating pay. Automation didn't erase the role—it compressed it.

This pattern is increasingly visible across sectors. In journalism, AI tools like BloombergGPT assist with market summaries. In law, firms like A&O Shearman are using Harvey, a GPT-based legal assistant. In local government, councils across the UK are piloting AI chatbots for resident queries. Sometimes these tools replace; sometimes they assist; often, they reshape the job and reduce how many people are needed to do it.

A job, then, is best understood as a bundle of tasks—some easily automated, others deeply human. AI's impact depends on which parts it touches. If it replaces rote work and enhances judgment, jobs may become better. But if it flattens complexity and lowers barriers to entry, jobs may become more precarious. The future of work isn't just about what AI can do. It's about what we choose to let it do—and how we structure the world around those choices.

AI AS AN EXPANSIONARY FORCE

History shows that tools designed to simplify life often expand industries rather than diminish them. The microwave didn't kill home cooking—it helped create the age of the celebrity chef. When DJing became more accessible thanks to free music-sharing platforms and user-friendly production tools, superstars like Avicii and Tiësto rose to fame. And when AI began defeating chess grandmasters, it didn't end the game—it expanded the number of recognized grandmasters from fewer than a hundred to nearly two thousand. Rather than eliminating work, new technologies tend to shift roles and titles around.

This brings us to Steve Wozniak's coffee challenge. The Apple co-founder posed a deceptively simple question:

"Can a robot walk into your house and make you a cup of coffee?" At first glance, it seems trivial. But consider what it requires: the robot must identify your house, unlock the door, recognize the coffee machine, understand how it works, select the right mug, adjust for your coffee preferences, and serve it without spilling—all while navigating an unpredictable, cluttered environment. The challenge highlights the gap between AI's ability to execute defined tasks and the broader complexities of real-world labor.

AI AS AN EQUALIZER

The great potential of AI is to enable more people to work using digital tools without special training. Just like ride-sharing services such as Uber allow drivers to navigate unfamiliar cities without memorizing maps, AI is expanding who can participate in the global economy by lowering barriers to entry.

When the World Economic Forum published its Future of Jobs report in 2025,[30] it estimated that the broadening of digital access was a much greater job creator than robots and autonomous systems were job destroyers. Similarly, Oxford academics Carl Benedikt Frey and Michael Osborne, writing in *The Economist*, argue that "technologies like AI tend to complement low-skilled workers rather than replace them, enabling tasks that were previously beyond their reach."[31] Platforms like Uber or DoorDash empower workers to leverage AI systems that would have been unimaginable a decade earlier. Likewise, non-technical entrepreneurs can now use AI tools to handle marketing, coding, or analytics, unlocking opportunities that once required specialized expertise.

This assistive dynamic aligns with the examples discussed earlier in the chapter. Tools like GitHub Copilot or LawGeex augment human capabilities, enabling professionals to focus on more complex, creative, or strategic aspects of their work. Just as a good assistant 'stands beside' rather than replaces, AI can help workers in diverse roles tackle challenges that demand improvisation, empathy, or cultural understanding.

THE REAL QUESTION: HOW WILL AI REDEFINE WORK?

The central lesson is this: rather than asking whether AI will create or destroy jobs, we should focus on how it will assist in redefining them. The economic impact of AI will be determined not just by technological capabilities but by how industries and societies choose to integrate it. Few roles, even those considered routine, are immune to the need for human improvisation and judgment. By enhancing our ability to navigate complexity, AI assistants can elevate how we approach work, enabling us to focus on what humans do best: making instinctual decisions based on partial information.

CONCLUSION: DETACHED EMPATHY

We tend to overestimate a doctor's personality as an indicator of their skill level. If they are outgoing, friendly, and tender, we tend to rate them higher than if they are arrogant, introverted, or aloof. Yet a doctor is not your friend—you seek them out for expertise, not companionship. A doctor who is too empathetic might avoid uncomfortable but necessary procedures or questions, missing essential diagnostic clues. In such cases, a more detached, objective approach can lead to better medical outcomes. This is one of many areas where an independent third party, like an AI tool, can intervene to ensure that certain standards are met.

Other examples include recruitment and hiring, where AI can reduce unconscious bias by evaluating candidates solely on qualifications, and sports officiating, where systems like Hawk-Eye in tennis ensure impartial decisions by removing human error. In education, AI-powered tools provide objective grading and personalized learning plans, free from the favoritism that can influence teachers. Similarly, in workplace performance reviews,

AI can focus on measurable outcomes rather than subjective impressions, offering fairer assessments. In these cases, AI acts as an impartial assistant, helping maintain high standards and ensuring decisions are based on data, not personal bias.

For centuries, we have relied solely on human judgment, often to our detriment. In fields like medicine, this dependence has led to misdiagnoses or overlooked warning signs, sometimes with fatal consequences. Biases, emotions, and subjective interpretations can cloud decision-making, whether in a doctor's office, a courtroom, or a hiring process. By introducing AI as an impartial assistant, we gain a tool that can complement human expertise, reduce errors, and ensure that decisions are guided by data-driven objectivity, ultimately leading to fairer and more reliable outcomes.

However, the increasing reliance on AI as an assistant also comes with risks, particularly the erosion of human expertise. In aviation, the US Federal Aviation Administration has long acknowledged pilots' skill erosion at the expense of automation.[32] Today, driving automation may be following a similar path. Automatic transmissions, for example, have made driving more convenient for decades, but many drivers now find it difficult—or even impossible—to operate a manual car when the need arises. As we increasingly rely on assistive technologies, from adaptive cruise control to active driver assistance to automated driving systems, drivers may lose the reflexes and adaptability required to handle emergencies. This highlights a broader challenge: balancing technological convenience with maintaining crucial human skills.

This challenge extends beyond skill erosion into deeper questions about human agency, particularly in domains like justice. Courtroom decisions, which profoundly affect lives, raise uncomfortable questions about AI's role. Could a machine, devoid of empathy or cultural understanding, deliver a verdict that truly serves justice? And even more critically: Should a machine deliver a verdict? AI may excel in analyzing evidence and identifying patterns, but justice is not solely about data—it is about human interpretation, moral nuance, and accountability.

Ian McEwan's novel *Machines Like Me* presents a chilling thought experiment on this very issue. In the story, an advanced AI named Adam turns in its human owner's friend for committing a violent act. Though the justice system fails to act on the crime, Adam sees no ambiguity—his programming compels him to report the wrongdoer. The result? The human, who had acted in a morally complex situation, is imprisoned, while Adam, incapable of understanding context, remains convinced of the correctness of his action.

This fictional dilemma is now colliding with reality. In 2025, the United Arab Emirates made headlines by issuing regulations that would allow AI to play a role in judicial rulings.[33] According to *The Hill*, the country is positioning itself as a global pioneer in 'AI-enhanced' legal decision-making, potentially integrating AI into both civil and criminal proceedings. The ambition is to improve efficiency and consistency. But the UAE is not a liberal democracy—freedom of expression is restricted, judicial independence is limited, and political dissent is often criminalized. In such a system, algorithmic 'justice' could entrench authoritarian control rather than promote fairness

The danger is not that AI will malfunction—but that it will work exactly as designed, enforcing rules with unflinching precision and no empathy. The result could be faster verdicts but colder, less human justice. When fairness becomes a calculation, we must ask: What exactly are we optimizing for?

The essence of justice often lies in its human voice, where a decision is not just a mechanical output but a reflection of society's values and principles. Automatic sentencing or AI-driven rulings risk undermining the trust and humanity that the justice system depends on. Without a human voice to weigh context and intent, we risk reducing justice to an algorithm, stripping it of the moral reasoning that underpins its legitimacy.

Balancing these dynamics requires careful thought. AI should enhance human capabilities, not replace them. Whether in the driver's seat or the courtroom, AI must serve as a guide and safeguard, ensuring consistency and clarity while leaving the final say (for the foreseeable future) to humans. This partnership preserves our ability to refine our skills, uphold our values, and navigate complex ethical landscapes—qualities no machine can replicate.

The assistant role of AI is not about replacing humans but augmenting our strengths, guiding us through complexities, and filling gaps in our objectivity. It provides both empathy and detachment when needed, ensuring a balance between understanding and impartiality. This duality highlights AI's evolving role—not just as a neutral tool, but as a dynamic collaborator, adapting to the situational needs of human decision-making.

As we move into the next chapter on AI as a creator, the question shifts: If AI can assist us with logic and impartiality, can it also contribute to the realms of art, innovation, and originality? What happens when AI is not just an enabler of human creativity but a participant in it?

CHAPTER THREE

AI AS A CREATOR

THE LAST STAND?

Vienna's Volkstheater is built in the historicist style that was popular in the late 1800s, where buildings were designed to look older than they are. The 'volk'-epithet reveals the original mission to expose a broad population, not just the elites, to popular and classical plays. It was here that a battle between man and machine took place in October 2024. British freestyle rapper Chris Turner had challenged ChatGPT, the world's most popular chatbot at the time, to a rap battle similar to the ones popularized in hip-hop circles, where the goal is to verbally assault, insult, and entertain your fellow participants, with the audience's cheers serving as a kind of real-time referee. As Turner warmed up beside the mic'd-up laptop, the audience wondered whether this would be the time and place where human creativity finally ceded victory to the machines.

While the 19th-century Luddites were blue-collar textile workers angry about their crafts being taken over by machines and 20th-century factory workers seeing their professions increasingly automated and robotized, the most profound concern in modern times has been whether AI can and will outshine humans in creative endeavors. If this had been a horror movie poster, the slogan would have been something ominous like "This time, the machines are coming for your precious creative jobs."

AI has already drawn first blood. Chatbots excel when it comes to lateral thinking. Research comparing ChatGPT-4 with 151 human participants on three divergent thinking tests found that the AI outperformed humans in creative tasks. These tests, aimed at evaluating the capacity to produce unique and inventive ideas, demonstrated that GPT-4 generated more original and detailed responses.[34, 35]

Katja Hofmann, a researcher at Microsoft, taught AI to play Bleeding Edge, a popular online role-playing game, by training it on 8.6 years of data. Within a very short time, it was the best player in the world, but, more importantly, it could generate new characters and gaming scenarios all by itself, based on its in-depth understanding of the game.[36]

This list will, by the time this book is published, have grown significantly longer and larger, showing how an activity previously believed to be a humans-only domain is not only automated but enriched by the speedy magic of machine learning. But we must ask ourselves, what exactly is creativity?

THE ORDERING OF INFORMATION

Consider yet again the box of Legos in my basement from the chapter about AI as a doer. Lego is seen as a creativity tool because of its versatility. Only your imagination limits what you can and cannot build, even with a small number of colorful bricks. Yet we only consider it creative once human hands have intentionally built something. We don't comment on the box itself, with its chaotic pile of pieces, as being creative, even though it contains all the same potential.

Similarly, a crashed Ferrari is worthless, while a new Ferrari commands a fortune. In one sense, that is strange, considering they both contain the same number of parts. A child banging on a piano has the same keys at his or her disposal as a master composer, but few would pay to hear the child hammering away. In contrast, the works of Bach or Chopin are viewed as timeless masterpieces.

These examples suggest that creativity isn't about the materials themselves—it's about how humans arrange, interpret, and transform them into something meaningful. Furthermore, we should question whether creativity is the process of making or the final result.

Take the renowned German painter Gerhard Richter, for example. When he paints, much of his creative process involves stepping back from the canvas and simply looking—sometimes for hours. He waits for a sense of 'rightness' to emerge, deciding whether what he has done resonates or requires change. Is the art in the act of painting or in the judgment that follows? If he stopped before making that final decision, would it still be considered art—or just paint on canvas?

This idea also resonates with film director James Cameron's comment about acting in the age of AI: "The machine could give you a plausible performance, but it won't give you the quirky moment of creation that an actor provides—that is particular to them and their life experience."[37]

His point underscores a crucial aspect of human creativity: unpredictability. Machines can replicate convincing outputs, but creativity often lives in the imperfections, surprises, and deeply personal interpretations that machines, at least for now, cannot generate.

Perhaps this distinguishes human creativity from mechanical production—the capacity to feel when something is right, make meaning from disorder, and inject something personal, impromptu, or even flawed, into the work.

This raises an unsettling question in the age of AI: Does it matter if something was created by a human or a machine, as long as the result moves us? Is the difference between a real and a fake plant significant—or does only the experience of seeing green leaves matter?

FLOWERS AND MUZAK

Imagine walking into the lobby of a hotel belonging to one of the larger chains. There's a reception and concierge, usually a group of chairs or couches, generic carpets, and some potted flowers. Imagine you have to wait to check in because of a short queue in front of the reception desk, so you sit on one of the beige couches. You look at the flowers and plants. They add a pleasant feeling and a certain connection to nature. They add to the relaxing, welcoming atmosphere the hotel chain wants its properties and brand to radiate. When the queue has shortened, and you walk to the reception desk, you pass one of the plants and let your fingertips graze its leaves. It's made of plastic. When you look closer, you realize all the plants and flowers are fake. Does it diminish your impression of the hotel lobby?

As you ride the elevator, the soft piano music follows you. It's vaguely familiar—an evergreen tune you've heard countless times in similar spaces. It creates a sense of calm, blending into the background. But what if you learned that the music wasn't performed by a real pianist but generated by a Muzak algorithm designed to produce endless hours of soothing soundscapes? Would that change how you feel about the music—or the hotel experience as a whole?

Now, consider the plants again. Imagine entering a prestigious gardening competition, presenting a stunning floral arrangement—and winning—only for the judges to discover later that your flowers were made of plastic. Would your victory still count? Would people consider your arrangement less beautiful, even if no one could tell the difference at first glance?

We see this tension in the arts, too. In a recent experiment on AI-generated art published by Astral Codex Ten, participants were asked to distinguish between human artworks and those made by AI. Many claimed to dislike AI-generated art strongly—but when tested, they couldn't reliably tell the difference. Even self-professed art enthusiasts frequently misidentify AI creations as being made by humans.[38]

This points to an uncomfortable truth: our biases shape how we value art and creativity. We often assume that AI-generated works are less valuable or authentic—but only when we know machines made them. Without that knowledge, many people appreciate AI-generated art just as much as human-made pieces.

Beyond artificial perfection lies a more profound question: Can machines ever replicate the unpredictable, intuitive spark that defines human creativity—or are their best efforts destined to remain lifelike but lifeless?

We see this tension play out in cultural competitions, too. What if you discovered that a Eurovision Song Contest winner was, in fact, a song generated by an AI?

Would it still be worthy of applause—or would you feel cheated, even if the song was catchy and well produced? The same goes for Spotify playlists: Would you enjoy your favorite playlist less if you found out it was entirely curated by an algorithm instead of a human DJ?

These examples reveal a deeper truth: context and expectations shape our judgments. We not only care about what something is but how it came to be. The knowledge that something was created by a human—or not—can change its value in our minds, even if the outcome itself remains identical.

Technology has always shaped the form creativity takes. Early movies commonly lasted around 90 minutes because theaters used multiple reels, each holding approximately 15 to 20 minutes of film, making this duration a practical standard based on reel constraints. Later, TV networks created 12-hour movies and called them series. Netflix expanded this idea with 48-hour stories labeled as seasons. TikTok took it in the opposite direction, creating 10-second 'movies' that collectively drew larger audiences than *Star Wars* or *Game of Thrones*.

Similarly, the limited bandwidth and cost of production limited radio programs to an hour or less only a few decades ago, whereas cheap digital recording tools and the infinite bandwidth of the World Wide Web enabled podcasters to create four-hour interviews and rants.

We live in a world of content inflation, with attention shrinking and becoming more valuable by each gigabyte produced.

What happens when AI generates entire seasons of TV shows, endlessly expanding narratives without human intervention? Would you care if your favorite show had no human writer behind it—as long as it remained entertaining? Would it even be 'a show' in the traditional sense—or something entirely new?

What if the future of podcasts is just a prompt? "I need a five-hour talk show about the origins of World War II to help me fall asleep, voiced by Morgan Freeman?"

Ultimately, this is about expectations. We accept—or even embrace—machine-generated content when we expect or desire it, as with TikTok or Spotify playlists. But when we assume human intent behind something and discover otherwise, it can feel like a breach of trust, even if the experience itself was positive.

This leads to a crucial question for the age of AI: Do we judge machines more harshly than humans? If a human gardener unknowingly used fake plants, we might forgive the mistake. If an algorithm did the same, would we be so lenient?

And perhaps the most profound question of all: Does intent matter in creativity? Is something inherently more valuable if we know a human meant to create it—or is that just another story we tell ourselves to assign meaning in a world increasingly shaped by machines?

THE IMPERFECTION ENGINE

"To err is human, it takes a computer to really screw it up," as a famous bumper sticker puts it. This tendency can be seen in how differently we treat accidental creativity in machines and people.

If a chatbot gives nonsensical answers, we call it 'hallucinating'—a serious flaw that undermines trust in AI systems. In humans, hallucinations are often associated with mental illness and carry a significant stigma. Yet we also recognize that imaginative leaps—whether from daydreams, altered states, or unconventional thinking—can sometimes lead to flashes of genius, artistic inspiration, or even moments perceived as divine insight. This duality underscores the complex relationship we have with non-rational cognition—and highlights how differently we judge it in machines versus ourselves.

Mike Fleiss had by the year 2000 become a laughing stock in Hollywood. Despite having created a hit TV show, he was broke, with two small kids and bills to pay. His show, *Who Wants to Marry a Multi-Millionaire?*, had become subject to controversy and lawsuits. One morning, an insight in the form of a feverish hallucination came to him. Nursing an actual fever, he lay in bed listening to his wife planning a high school reunion. What if he created a reality show about high school reunions? That idea became a stepping stone for a much bigger idea: What if I create a game show where women compete to find a soul mate? *The Bachelor*, one of the most successful ideas in TV history, had been born. "90% of what's on the show today, I saw it in five minutes,"[39] Fleiss would later say as he described the flash of insight. When humans hallucinate, magic can happen.

Some of the most iconic creative works and scientific breakthroughs were born from such moments of 'mental drift.' Fleetwood Mac's Christine McVie famously dreamed the melody and lyrics to "Songbird," while Paul McCartney woke up one morning with "Yesterday" fully formed in his mind, rushing to the piano to play what he thought must be someone else's song. David Bowie claimed that "Life on Mars?" came to him while staring out the window of a bus, his mind wandering through surreal landscapes.

Creativity through hallucination isn't limited to music or art. History is full of groundbreaking inventions born from strange visions and unexpected leaps of thought:

- **The Periodic Table:** Dmitri Mendeleev, the chemist, reportedly saw the structure of the periodic table in a dream, where chemical elements arranged themselves in a logical order. He woke up and wrote it down—and the modern periodic table was born.
- **The Sewing Machine:** Inventor Elias Howe struggled to design a working sewing machine until he

dreamed of being captured by tribal warriors carrying spears with holes in the tips. He awoke and realized that placing the needle's eye near its tip could solve his design problem.
- **Benzene's Structure**: Chemist August Kekulé discovered the ring-like structure of benzene after daydreaming of a snake biting its own tail—a symbol from mythology known as the ouroboros. This mental image helped revolutionize organic chemistry.

Even in business, intuition-driven 'hallucinations' have led to iconic creations. Burger King founder Jim McLamore reportedly came up with both the recipe and name for the Whopper hamburger while driving drunk through Florida one night—a questionable context, but a defining moment for the fast-food world.

The line between visionary creativity and chaotic nonsense is often razor-thin. What machines produce as 'errors' can, at times, resemble the leaps of intuition or provocation we admire in human creativity. Of course, not all mistakes are created equal—an obviously wrong answer is just wrong, whether it comes from a chatbot or a person. But in more ambiguous cases, the same idea dismissed as an AI glitch might be hailed as genius if it came from a human since we instinctively assign meaning and intention to human creativity, assuming there's a conscious mind behind it. But could machines one day produce their own "Yesterday" or *The Bachelor* through a similar process—one we currently dismiss as a glitch or hallucination?

Will the future of creativity depend not on eliminating machine hallucinations but on learning to interpret them, just as we've long done with our wandering minds?

These stories of inspiration born from dreams, daydreams, and even mistakes highlight something profound about human creativity: the process matters as much as the outcome.

The songs, inventions, and ideas we celebrate didn't emerge fully formed from thin air—they came from wandering, unpredictable processes. The brilliance of Paul McCartney's "Yesterday" wasn't just in the melody he woke up with—it was in the months he spent perfecting its lyrics and chords. Mendeleev's dream of the periodic table might have provided the core insight, but it took years of scientific work to fill in the gaps.

This emphasis on process is something machines struggle with. We value the creative journey because it reflects human effort, struggle, and intention. The accidental discovery of penicillin was revolutionary precisely because Alexander Fleming recognized its potential and followed through with disciplined scientific research. Machines, on the other hand, generate results without the backstory of effort, failure, and persistence—qualities we instinctively associate with meaningful creation.

As musician Nick Cave reflects in *The Red Hand Files*, the process of creation is sacred—not because it's efficient, but because it's slow, difficult, and deeply personal. In response to whether AI could write meaningful songs, Cave wrote:

> Songs arise out of suffering, by confronting the difficult stuff of life. It requires time, effort, and a kind of sacred struggle. ChatGPT ... has no inner being, no history of struggle. It's a tool, not a creator. A song is a living thing.[40]

CHAPTER THREE: AI AS A CREATOR

Similarly, formulating sentences is not a nuisance for a novel writer but a fundamental part of storytelling in prose. As *The New Yorker* journalist Ted Chiang describes it:

> Art is something that results from making a lot of choices. This might be easiest to explain if we use fiction writing as an example. When you are writing fiction, you are—consciously or unconsciously—making a choice about almost every word you type; to oversimplify, we can imagine that a ten-thousand-word short story requires something on the order of ten thousand choices. When you give a generative-A.I. program a prompt, you are making relatively few choices; if you supply a hundred-word prompt, you have made on the order of a hundred choices.
>
> If an A.I. generates a ten-thousand-word story based on your prompt, it has to fill in for all of the choices that you are not making. There are various ways it can do this. One is to take an average of the choices that other writers have made, as represented by text found on the Internet; that average is equivalent to the least interesting choices possible, which is why A.I.-generated text is often really bland. Another is to instruct the program to engage in style mimicry, emulating the choices made by a specific writer, which produces a highly derivative story. In neither case is it creating interesting art.[41]

This reverence for process goes beyond art into how we define success itself. In *Why Greatness Cannot Be Planned*,[42] Kenneth O. Stanley and Joel Lehman argue that fixating too much on specific, measurable goals can limit creativity and block the paths to unexpected success.

An infant does not learn through objectives but by curiously exploring the world around it. Creativity isn't a straight line from idea to execution—it's a chaotic, often frustrating process filled with dead ends and surprising detours. But those detours are often where true breakthroughs happen.

Imagine if *Ulysses*, James Joyce's groundbreaking novel published in 1922, had been written by AI. Its fragmented, stream-of-consciousness style—revolutionizing modern literature—might have been dismissed as a glitch or a malfunction. We would have called the manuscript 'broken.' But because it came from a human being, we view it as an intentional masterpiece—a deliberate reshaping of how stories could be told. The perceived intent behind the work fundamentally changes how we judge its value.

Machines can produce complex, even brilliant, works—but without intent, we struggle to assign meaning. We look for a creator's story, a personal struggle, or a more profound reason behind what was made. If those elements are missing, even the most stunning art or music can feel hollow—like something was lost in translation.

This brings us to a crucial question for the age of AI: Can the process still matter if no human is involved? If machines can create instantaneously, bypassing the struggles we see as essential to creativity, will we still value what they make—or will something intangible be lost along the way?

EXPLORATION OR TRANSFORMATION?

In the previous chapters on doing and assisting, the focus has been on problems to solve. At first glance, creativity seems different. A person writing a poem isn't solving a 'poetry problem,' and a song isn't composed to 'fix' a song gap. "The end of a melody is not its goal," as philosopher Friedrich Nietzsche put it.

Creativity isn't a single task but a process of smaller, interlinked microtasks. A poem has rhythm, structure, and carefully chosen words to evoke a particular feeling or vision. The poet might even be trying to resolve an inner tension, experimenting through multiple drafts to find the right expression. The same applies to other creative pursuits, from composing pop songs to crafting theatrical scripts. More importantly, creativity isn't limited to the arts. Inventors, managers, plumbers, and schoolteachers all apply creativity when faced with unexpected challenges or when generating new ideas. Seen this way, creativity can be framed as a process of solving interconnected microtasks within an existing framework—what we might call 'exploratory creativity.'

We explore possibilities within familiar structures, uncovering new combinations or patterns. A poet searches for synonyms for rain, a plumber considers alternative ways to fix a broken pipe, and a teacher designs a series of math exercises. Each works creatively but within the boundaries of known rules, tools, and expectations—a process of exploring and refining rather than redefining the entire system. AI excels as a tool for exploratory creativity because it can rapidly generate, filter, and combine possibilities, acting as a collaborative partner in tasks like brainstorming, prototyping, and refining ideas.

Sanofi, a French pharmaceutical company, has integrated AI into its drug development processes through initiatives like the AI-powered app Plai, which was developed in partnership with Aily Labs. Plai compiles and processes internal data from various departments, creating bespoke "what if" scenarios to guide decision-making, thereby enhancing strategic planning and operational efficiency.[43] This application of AI enables Sanofi to explore vast datasets, identify novel drug candidates, and streamline clinical trials. In music production, AI tools like Amper Music or AIVA can generate melody variations, helping composers explore new harmonic structures. AI-powered platforms like Adobe's Sensei suggest pattern combinations or color palettes in fashion design, sparking new design ideas. Even in writing, AI-driven tools such as Sudowrite assist authors by proposing alternative phrases or narrative directions, supporting creative exploration within a chosen literary style.

In all these cases, AI is an exploratory co-creator, expanding the range of possibilities while working within the established frameworks of each creative domain. This approach offers low-cost instant creativity, enabling humans to rapidly explore countless possibilities without the time, expense, or labor traditionally required—making experimentation more accessible and innovation more scalable across industries.

While exploration can yield remarkable results, true revolution happens when we break the framework entirely. Consider the origin story of ON running shoes. Faced with the challenge of creating a new kind of running sole, the founders experimented with an unlikely material: pieces of garden hose. They cut the hoses into sections and attached them to a basic shoe sole, discovering that the resulting structure provided a unique cushioning and propulsion effect. This unconventional experiment eventually led to ON's signature CloudTec sole, a revolutionary design in the running shoe industry.[44]

This is 'transformational creativity'—the kind that shatters existing frameworks, rewrites the rules and forges something the world has never seen. It's the leap from the familiar to the unimaginable.

Unlike Sanofi's exploration, discovering the Swedish drug Orfadin was a stroke of transformational creativity from an unexpected scientific collision. A failed herbicide from an Australian agrochemical company, designed to suppress weeds, unexpectedly held the key to treating a deadly genetic disorder in children. When two doctors in Gothenburg connected the molecule's biochemical effects to the enzyme responsible for Tyrosinemia, they crossed the boundaries of agricultural and medical research—transforming a discarded weed-killing chemical into a life-saving drug. This was no systematic search—it was an unpredictable breakthrough that rewrote medical science.[45]

What we humans call creativity might ultimately be a search problem—where solutions and answers are found in unexpected places. In *Why Greatness Cannot Be Planned*,[46] Stanley and Lehman argue for Novelty Search—a strategy where progress comes from seeking the unexplored, not optimizing for predefined targets. This mirrors how Orfadin emerged—not through a focused search of familiar and adjacent medical treatments, but from an agricultural company's unrelated work on herbicides on the other side of the world.

Such breakthroughs aren't just about exploration —they also require 'bisociation,' a concept Arthur Koestler introduced in *The Act of Creation*.[47] Bisociation happens when two unrelated domains collide, creating something fundamentally new. One example of this is biomimicry, designing solutions inspired by natural phenomena, like Velcro (inspired by burrs) or self-cleaning surfaces (modeled after lotus leaves). Entire research fields have been created by these collisions, from geophysics to neuroscience.

The same principle appears across industries and art forms, reshaping entire fields through unexpected collisions of ideas. ON Shoes revolutionized shoe design by discarding conventional materials and inventing a completely new cushioning system. Similarly, NVIDIA's graphic processing units, originally designed for gaming, were repurposed for machine learning, enabling breakthroughs in AI research and transforming NVIDIA into the world's most valuable semiconductor company.

In literature, James Joyce's *Ulysses* shattered traditional narrative structures with its stream-of-consciousness style, reshaping modern fiction. In contemporary art, Tracey Emin's *My Bed* transformed personal vulnerability into high art by presenting her disheveled bed as an autobiographical installation, redefining what could be considered art. These creators didn't refine existing frameworks—they broke them, expanded the possibilities of their fields, and left behind entirely new landscapes for others to explore.

CREATIVITY IS ABOUT UNCERTAINTY, NOT JUST PROBABILITY

While AI thrives on probabilities, human creativity lives in uncertainty. AI excels when rules are clear and probabilities can be calculated, making it powerful in tasks where outcomes can be modeled and optimized. But transformational creativity—the kind that rewrites the rules entirely—exists in a space where outcomes can't be predicted or systematized.

Claude Debussy once said: "Works of art make rules; rules do not make works of art." Creativity defies formulaic thinking. In fact, 'formulaic' is one of the harshest insults you can give an artist. When humans create, they often do so by embracing the unpredictable, venturing into the unknown, and discovering meaning along the way. AI can rearrange known elements based on probabilities—but only humans can create something entirely unexpected by embracing uncertainty.

This tension becomes clearer when we return to the idea of Muzak and plastic plants from earlier in this chapter. Both are designed to fit in, providing a sense of comfort and familiarity—but without true creativity. A plastic plant can't wilt, and Muzak won't miss a note, but neither will surprise or transform us. Their perfection makes them predictable—and ultimately forgettable.

The same principle applies to products in the marketplace. Business thinker Clayton Christensen's famous 'Jobs to Be Done' theory explains how we 'hire' products to perform specific tasks in our lives. We accept robot bartenders in fast-food chains like McDonald's, where speed and consistency matter more than personal service. But in a high-end cocktail bar, where a skilled bartender crafts bespoke drinks and engages in unpredictable conversation, automation feels out of place. The job a product is hired to perform determines the level of automation we accept. We hire Muzak to fit in but pay good money to enjoy the uniqueness of a Dua Lipa concert. While we expect it to be good, even stellar, her ways of delivering this experience are uncertain, not formulaic. In the realm of freestyle rap, where improvisation and verbal dexterity are essential, uncertainty reigns. Returning to the rap battle between Chris Turner and ChatGPT: while the AI generated a few clever lines through probabilistic reasoning, its rhymes lacked the wit, emotion, and presence of a human performer navigating the unknown in real time. The ability to think on one's feet, react unpredictably, and—above all—connect with an audience remains uniquely human. This is why the showdown in Vienna was a resounding success for Turner and a failure for the mic'd-up laptop.

AI output is, by definition, probable and plausible—essentially 'average.' In contexts where average works, such as customer service emails, AI shines. However, in domains where originality, emotion, and distinctiveness are paramount—like art, music, videos, insights, briefs, or intelligence—'average' is often worthless.

Uncertainty isn't just a feature of art—it's central to some of the world's most complex and impactful endeavors.

ENTREPRENEURIAL UNCERTAINTY

Think about entrepreneurship. The word contains the French *entre* meaning 'in between.' Entrepreneurs explore spaces left unexplored or underserved, whether it is Dietrich Matescitz adapting the Thai tonic Krating Daeng to Western palates and selling it under the brand name Red Bull, or Melitta Bentz using blotting paper taken from her son's school notebook to invent the first coffee filter. Entrepreneurs thrive on so-called 'epistemic uncertainty,' the kind of uncertainty that arises from a lack of current knowledge or statistical evidence.

DIPLOMATIC UNCERTAINTY

Epistemic uncertainty can be seen in the work of skilled diplomats like Dag Hammarskjöld. When he became Secretary-General of the United Nations in 1953, Hammarskjöld inherited a tense situation: the Korean War had ended, but 11 American pilots were still being held as prisoners by China. The crisis unfolded during a time of Cold War hostilities, McCarthyism, and profound mistrust between superpowers.

Rather than succumb to the pressures of the era, Hammarskjöld adopted a nuanced approach rooted in patience and discretion. As the article notes, "he avoided the publicity which would have drawn political vultures to the scene." Instead, Hammarskjöld undertook quiet negotiations, communicating directly with China through informal channels. He traveled to Beijing in January 1955 to meet Premier Zhou Enlai, a move that emphasized respect and a willingness to engage personally—a stark contrast to the public ultimatums and coercive rhetoric that might have been expected.[48]

By working behind the scenes and building trust over time, Hammarskjöld managed to secure the release of the American prisoners without heightening tensions between the United States and China. His approach demonstrated that in diplomacy, uncertainty is not an obstacle to be overcome but a reality to be navigated. Hammarskjöld's success lay in his ability to maintain flexibility, interpret subtle signals, and find common ground in an otherwise polarized and volatile world. This episode underscores how diplomacy often operates in a space where rigid strategies falter. Hammarskjöld's legacy shows how careful, deliberate action can transform uncertainty into opportunity.

DESIRED UNCERTAINTY

Think about riding Disney's iconic roller coaster, Space Mountain: you're hurtling through darkness, unable to anticipate the next turn, drop, or sudden acceleration. It's precisely the absence of certainty—the inability to see what's coming—that transforms this experience from a simple amusement park ride into a thrilling adventure. The excitement lies not in predictability, but in surprise.

In fact, 'uncertainty' itself might be the wrong word, as it implies that certainty is the ideal state. Yet we frequently crave the opposite of order, structure, careful planning, and clear expectations. We seek out experiences that shake us up, catch us off-guard, or jolt us into awareness—whether it's a jump scare in a horror movie, an unexpected flavor in a carefully plated dish at a restaurant, or a spontaneous conversation sparked by a chance meeting at a conference.

SCIENTIFIC UNCERTAINTY

Science, too, thrives on uncertainty and surprise. In the 1960s, Derek de Solla Price coined the term 'mavericity' to describe the unorthodox, radical thinking required to uncover new truths and drive genuine progress—not just incremental improvements. Yet today, much of science is dominated by analysis: meticulously parsing probabilities, seeking predictable patterns, and incrementally refining existing knowledge. Analysts map the trees in the forest with impressive accuracy, meticulously documenting every branch and leaf, and often identify new findings through unknown or previously undocumented details.

But it is visionary thinkers who imagine entirely new paths through that forest—and beyond it.

True scientific innovation often doesn't come simply from interpreting data; it emerges from imagining possibilities previously considered unlikely or impossible. While analysis leads to new insights within existing fields, visionary creativity in science generates entirely new programs, disciplines, and paradigms—quantum physics, biotechnology, and artificial intelligence itself were born from precisely this willingness to embrace radical uncertainty.

The future of science depends on cultivating more than just skillful analysts—those who chart what 'is.' It demands visionaries who dare to explore what 'could be,' who look at uncertainty and see not chaos, but opportunity.

David Spiegelhalter captures this critical tension in *The Art of Uncertainty*:

> [The] constant state of uncertainty is an essential part of the human condition. It may be mundane ('what's for lunch?') or existential ('will there be a catastrophic global war in the next hundred years?')[...] [and] tolerance of uncertainty can vary hugely between people—some might get a sense of excitement from unpredictability, while others feel chronic anxiety.[49]

CONCLUSION: THE H-FACTOR

The philosopher Hubert Dreyfus, in *What Computers Can't Do* (1972), argued that human creativity arises from levels of knowledge that machines cannot replicate:

- **Biological (innate abilities)**
  Newborns naturally recognize faces and respond to voices, forming the foundation for social bonding. Machines, in contrast, must be explicitly programmed or trained to interpret facial expressions or vocal tones—they lack our hardwired abilities.

- **Implicit (skills learned by doing)**
  Riding a bicycle is a classic example of an implicit skill. Once mastered, it becomes second nature, intuitively adaptable across various situations. Humans naturally generalize these skills, intuiting that one learned behavior can apply—in modified form—to another scenario.

  One of the primary goals in developing increasingly sophisticated AI is achieving this same ability

to generalize. Ideally, an AI could 'hypothesize' that task B shares similarities with task A and then intelligently test modifications of the original approach to accomplish the new task. However, such skill transfer presents challenges. While humans can intuitively adjust, machines typically require precise rules or vast datasets to safely generalize skills. After all, it's impractical—and undesirable—to crash multiple Jet Model B aircraft just to successfully adapt an autopilot system trained exclusively on Jet Model A.

Thus, a critical frontier for AI is developing ways to safely and effectively generalize learned skills without requiring extensive trial and error or explicit instructions for each new scenario.

- **Deliberative (logical reasoning)**
Machines excel at tasks requiring systematic, step-by-step reasoning, such as solving complex equations or analyzing medical images. Yet they perform these tasks without genuine understanding. For instance, a diagnostic algorithm might detect tumors with remarkable accuracy but cannot explain why a certain pattern indicates malignancy. This limitation creates the 'black-box' problem: machines cannot justify or clearly explain their conclusions, complicating trust—particularly in high-stakes fields like medicine.

A human radiologist, by contrast, integrates implicit and deliberative knowledge, noticing subtle anomalies beyond the machine's training data, prompting further investigation and potentially catching critical issues a machine might overlook.

The same challenge applies to highly automated driving systems. While AI-driven vehicles can perform impressively under normal conditions, functional safety standards demand that autonomous systems mitigate not only known risks but also unknown or unforeseen dangers—precisely the type of risks that cannot be anticipated through black-box algorithms alone. Human drivers intuitively sense when something feels 'off,' adapting swiftly to unpredictable road conditions. For autonomous vehicles, this ability to detect, reason through, and respond appropriately to unknown risks remains a crucial hurdle.

Thus, the future of deliberative AI depends significantly on solving this black-box problem: ensuring machines not only make accurate decisions but also meaningfully explain their reasoning, making them trustworthy partners in critical domains like medicine and transportation.

- **Self-conscious (reflection and meta-thinking)**
  So it is with our own past. It is a labor in vain to attempt to recapture it: all the efforts of our intellect must prove futile. The past is hidden somewhere outside the realm, beyond the reach of intellect, in some material object (in the sensation which that material object will give us) which we do not suspect. And as for that object, it depends on chance whether we come upon it or not before we ourselves must die.[50]

Reflecting on past experiences, as illustrated in Proust's *In Search of Lost Time*, involves a level of meta-awareness machines lack. The taste of a madeleine triggers not just memory but profound reflection on life's connections. Writing a memoir, for example, synthesizes emotions and experiences into a coherent narrative—an act of meaning-making that remains beyond the reach of any algorithm.

Creativity doesn't just transform materials—it transforms experience. Consider Mike Posner, who channeled feelings of disconnection into his global hit "I Took a Pill in Ibiza," or Eric Clapton, who turned his grief into the timeless "Tears in Heaven." Creativity is often born from life's lowest points, where we create not for success but to turn pain into something transcendent.

Not every creative act needs to succeed by conventional standards. A personal blog with few readers, a hand-painted mural, or a song never played on the radio still holds meaning. As Douglas Hofstadter argues in *Gödel, Escher, Bach*, even if AI surpasses human intelligence, it will struggle with "art, beauty, and simplicity"—qualities tied to human meaning-making. Machines may outthink us, but their creations lack the elusive human spark.

The Pixar film *Ratatouille* captures this sentiment beautifully with the declaration, "Anyone can cook." This is not just a feel-good slogan but a profound statement about creativity. It asks: Is creativity an innate talent reserved for a select few or something anyone can access in the right context? The answer lies in what we might call the H-Factor—a mysterious human quality that links experience and expression. It is why scriptwriters in the early 2020s protested against AI being trained on their work without fair compensation, holding signs like "ChatGPT doesn't have childhood trauma." Creativity stems from lived experience, not just data. It's a contact sport learned through the hands, the heart, and the gut.

Imperfection is often the hallmark of this authenticity. A homemade cabinet, though lopsided, reflects the love and effort poured into its making. In a world increasingly driven by precision, imperfection reminds us of the value of authenticity. Anyone can create in their own way, bringing unique meaning to the process.

AI, meanwhile, is not a creator but a tool. It can amplify creativity, acting as a grammar-checker on steroids—or LSD given the proneness to hallucinate—an idea generator, or a brainstorming partner and DJ of ideas. It's a companion that expands possibilities without replacing the essential human role in making sense of them. After all, ideas come through us, not just from us. In this way, we are all generative AIs, recombining our vast experiences, emotions, and influences into something new and meaningful.

The H-Factor also explains why slowness is key to human pleasure—why we savor a glass of red wine in Lisbon, or linger over a painting, or lose ourselves in a novel. As Woody Allen quipped, "I took a speed-reading course and read *War and Peace* in 20 minutes. It's about Russia." You can consume information quickly, but you can't speed-read meaning. We would be wise to remember this in our TLDR[51] world, where depth and understanding are often sacrificed on the altar of speedy shallowness.

Yet our inherently human inability to communicate concisely or precisely also introduces significant challenges—particularly evident among Gen Z, who navigate a world dominated by rapid digital communication. Misunderstandings and confusion abound without communication or when nuance and context are lost in the quest for brevity, straining personal relationships, scientific discovery, and business interactions. The same self-conscious reflection that deepens creativity can also obscure straightforward communication, complicating our connections even as it enriches our experience.

Ultimately, creativity is fundamentally human, embracing imperfection and transforming life's uncertainty into something meaningful. Machines calculate probabilities, but humans live in uncertainty—and create from it. The H-Factor keeps us connected to ourselves, to each other, and to the infinite world of ideas waiting to be imagined. Because, in the end, creativity is not just what we make—it's how we make sense of being alive.

PART 2

WHOA!

Here comes the reality check! As AI moves from experiments to real-world adoption, it runs into friction. We've been here before. Electricity, the internet, and vehicle automation all promised radical change—yet institutions resisted, technological hurdles appeared, infrastructure needs limited growth, companies hesitated, and societies adapted far more slowly than expected. AI is no different.

What happens when AI collides with education systems designed for stability, not disruption? When powerful incumbents see it as a threat rather than an opportunity? When entire industries realize that integrating AI means rethinking everything, not just upgrading their tools?

The challenge ahead isn't about what AI can do. It's about whether we're willing—and able—to change alongside it. This requires embracing a little of the unknown at the risk of upending social norms to find a pathway to greater good. Guardrails are critical but only to make sure that technologies are poised to transparently advance the greater good over what almost will always will be costs to disruption.

CHAPTER FOUR
WILL WE LET AI CHANGE US?

WHERE'S THE REVOLUTION?

Imagine a classroom where every single student has their own personal tutor, adapted not only to their skill level but who also speaks in a tone of voice and with a choice of words best suited to their individual learning style. In short, a hyper-individualized learning environment. Yes, this is already possible with the AI chatbots on the market. And yes, it has proven superior. A famous Harvard study compared college students' learning and their perceptions when content is presented through an AI-powered tutor compared with an active learning class, where students interact and ask questions, not just participate passively. Not only did the AI-tutored students learn more than twice as much in less time but they also reported feeling more motivated and engaged.[52]

The transformative potential of AI in education isn't confined to elite institutions. In Edo State, Nigeria, a six-week after-school program utilizing generative AI tools like Microsoft Copilot led to remarkable improvements[53] in English language proficiency among first-year secondary students. Participants not only outperformed their peers in English assessments but also demonstrated enhanced digital literacy and AI knowledge. Notably, these students excelled in end-of-year exams across various subjects, indicating that AI-assisted learning, if integrated effectively, can have a profound impact even in resource-constrained settings.

In other words, AI is a silver bullet for education. But, as MIT's Head of AI Education and Innovation David Dixon, points out: "The fear is that we won't let AI change education enough. Not because it can't but because we won't let it."[54]

You may recall that we had the same discussions about the potential of the internet in classrooms. YouTube-enabled math tutoring would empower African children, Wikipedia was the best—and longest—textbook ever invented, and it was free. Children would no longer be constrained to the shortcomings of a single teacher but would be free to roam around the infinite knowledge of cyberspace. Fast forward to today where schools still rely on teachers and classrooms, connection speeds are patchy or non-existent, school laptops are inferior to what kids have at home, while smartphones and social media are increasingly banned, citing distraction or mental health concerns. Why would things turn out differently this time around?

FLASH WITHOUT THE BANG

In the fast-changing AI landscape, it is impossible to be an expert. In the words of technology author Ethan Mollick:

> *As someone who is pretty good at keeping up with AI, I can barely keep up with it all. That leads me to believe that very few other people are keeping up, either. So, on one hand, don't feel bad you aren't on top of it all. On the other hand, it means no one has the whole picture now.*[55]

What the first three chapters of this book showed was the speed with which AI makes us go "Wow!" But speed is only a signifier for capitalistic innovation. It is intended to dazzle and attract attention and most importantly capital.

Established corporations, on the other hand—especially if they have been around for a while—do not have the same urge, or need, to impress.

Societal institutions work at an even slower pace.

As a result, the "Wow!" phase of AI has yet to translate into meaningful economic gains.

Generative AI tools have succeeded as consumer-facing products, but many other AI models fail to deliver scalable, real-world applications. Economist Daron Acemoglu argues that AI will likely automate only about 5% of tasks in the near future, leading to a GDP boost of just 1%—a nontrivial but modest effect. One reason for this limited impact is that AI struggles with complex, unpredictable environments that demand human intuition and adaptability.[56]

One of the main reasons for this was captured by the chief data reporter at *The Financial Times*. While AI can easily write essays, pass law school admission tests and MBA finals, it struggles with the messiness of real-world jobs: carrying out the duties of an executive assistant, travel agent or book-keeping clerk—all computer-based jobs requiring entry level skills—is still beyond the capabilities of even cutting-edge AIs. They struggle to keep track of multiple streams of information, respond to a dynamic environment, work with unclear or changing goals and multitask. These unstructured workflows are a far cry from coding tests and exam questions.[57]

Furthermore, Acemoglu's research also highlights that AI is currently being deployed in ways that reinforce existing power structures rather than focusing on creating broad economic gains. Companies often focus on automation that reduces costs rather than on applications that boost worker productivity or foster new industries. This dynamic limits AI's ability to drive transformative economic change, confining its effects to specific areas rather than creating new industries.

Frey and Osborne note that most generative models "have largely failed to make it into the application layer as breakout products,"[58] not because of a lack of potential but due to the complexities of adapting AI to unpredictable, nuanced environments. For instance, companies piloting AI for complex tasks—like autonomous decision-making or supply chain management—often encounter unexpected hurdles: biased training datasets, lack of interoperability, limited repeatability, infrastructure or computational limitations, or resistance from human stakeholders. While AI excels at producing outputs quickly, its integration into messy, real-world systems remains a significant challenge.

This challenge is further reflected in workforce behavior and organizational adoption trends. According to Salesforce's Workforce Index,[59] nearly half of employees admitted to hiding their use of AI tools from their bosses. This suggests a gap in trust, training, or policy alignment—highlighting the disconnect between AI's potential and its practical workplace deployment. Similarly, a 2024 NTT DATA survey[60] found that many organizations are shifting their mindset about AI, emphasizing structured implementation over experimental 'play.' The survey underscores that while generative AI is no longer viewed as a toy, its practical value hinges on integrating it with clear guidance and measurable outcomes.

For now, the economic impact of AI remains muted. According to the United States Census Bureau, "only 6% of businesses use AI to produce goods and services. Output and labor-productivity growth, meanwhile, remain far below the soaring heights of the computer age in the 1990s." Without overcoming these barriers to integration and scaling, AI's transformative promise risks being delayed—even indefinitely through a growing risk of another AI winter:

HOW TO MAKE AI USEFUL

Customers stop paying top dollar for AI products; investors close their purses. Journalists begin more critically appraising the landscape. And because everyone feels burned (or embarrassed), things slide into an overly negative cycle: Even the computer scientists and inventors with legitimately interesting new paths for AI can't easily get funding to pursue them. This lasts for years.[61]

THE LONG AND WINDING ROAD

There is a reason financial speculation has been dubbed 'astrology for dudes.' It may be exciting to guess what the next world will look like and what its financial and technical winners will be, but these guesses are often wrong. In the past decade, we have seen bubbles form and collapse in legalized cannabis stocks and the metaverse, an arcane technological trend featuring online virtual worlds and currencies which McKinsey, a consultancy, estimated would be worth upwards of USD 5 trillion by 2030.[62] We distinguished in the introduction of this book between bubbles and balloons, where the former pops and disappears, while the latter can deflate, reinflate, and rise to ever greater heights. It is tempting to believe that what categorizes a speculative trend as one or the other is inherent at the creation—that every bubble is just a tulip bulb and every balloon a society-bettering utility. But if we don't let arguably useful technology infuse our society and its institutions, we are doomed to a cyclical world of sameness, even decline, interspersed with entertaining short-term gimmicks—think dot.com stocks or Floridian real estate—once per decade. To go from the spectacle of new technology into the long-windedness of institutional change—"wrestling with all the boring shit" as one of our interviewees put it—are two completely different activities. And they have historically taken a lot of time.

The wheel—the proverbial 'best invention ever'—was invented in Mesopotamia around 3500 BCE, but it took another couple of centuries to put the pottery wheels on vehicles, in the shape of ox carts. Then it took another thousand years to move from solid wooden to spoked wheels. We had to wait for the Romans to build roads and invent chariots to significantly speed up transport times, and it took until Dunlop invented rubber tires in 1888 to make rides fast and smooth.

Talking about Romans, they had some insights into steam power but used it to power a small toy called the aeolipile. To use it for industrial use took another thousand years or so.

The printing press in the mid-1400s took decades to spread from its native Germany to across European cities.

Even electricity took over 40 years to transform manufacturing.

We could, of course, argue here that 'this time it's different,' pointing to the speed at which radio, cable TV, and smartphones have been spreading around the world—mere years and decades, not centuries or millennia. But even these more recent, fast-spreading technologies had foundational periods of slow, incremental progress before their explosive adoption. The radio, for instance, was made possible by decades of experimentation with electromagnetic waves, culminating in Marconi's first transatlantic transmission in 1901.

Commercial broadcasting wouldn't take off until the 1920s, and it was another generation before it became ubiquitous. Similarly, the smartphone's seemingly overnight success was built on decades of development in semiconductors, wireless communication, and touch interfaces—none of which was inevitable or linear in its adoption. Time takes time. And minds change slowly, if at all. History shows that new technologies rarely integrate seamlessly into society. Not only do they take time to mature but they also contend with entrenched ways of thinking. Just as past innovations were held back by outdated mindsets, AI will face resistance—not just in adoption but in how we use it. We may not even recognize the ways in which our assumptions about AI reflect older, flawed ideas that should have been discarded long ago. To truly benefit from AI, we may first need to embrace the need to unlearn old habits, but as the saying goes, old habits die hard.

UNLEARNING

Bad ideas can linger for decades, leaving a lasting imprint. Take 'prevention by extension,' a dental procedure from the late 1800s. G. V. Black, the so-called father of modern dentistry, believed that not only cavities but also adjacent healthy tooth structure should be removed to prevent future decay. Given the absence of fluoride at the time, it seemed reasonable. But in practice, it led to unnecessary, even destructive dental work, often causing premature tooth loss—an approach that persisted until the 1980s.

The same pattern played out with lobotomies—a gruesome practice that somehow earned a Nobel Prize—and leaded gasoline, both of which endured for much of the 20th century before finally being consigned to the trash heap of history. The reason is that dentists and doctors who had been taught the merits of drilling into healthy teeth or cutting off the frontal lobe of patients with mental illness had to retire before new ideas could flourish. Similarly, putting lead into gasoline was a cheap way to improve performance in the 1920s, and we had to wait for the invention of catalytic converters to abolish it. To repeat what we stated in the introduction, digital technology evolved at the pace of Moore's Law, but mindsets change at a glacial, generational pace.

If we apply this to artificial intelligence, we can certainly see how it could be an efficient teaching tool or co-writer. But there are many question marks that still surround its efficacy. In a randomized clinical trial including 50 physicians, the use of AI did not significantly enhance diagnostic reasoning performance compared with the availability of only conventional resources.[63] Similarly, chatbots—being eager to please their users—have a nasty tendency to make things up. Daniel Litt, a math professor at the University of Toronto, found this out when he investigated whether democratized access to mathematics, thanks to the internet, had increased the rate of important math research done by young people. His findings were alarming but also informative as to the flaws of AI chatbots.

When Litt asked a popular AI chatbot for examples of breakthrough mathematical work published by young researchers in recent years, the chatbot provided a confident-sounding list of impressive results. The only problem? Many of these discoveries never happened. The chatbot had simply hallucinated achievements, fabricating research and attributing breakthroughs to real mathematicians who had never actually made those claims.[64]

This highlights a critical issue with LLMs: their tendency to prioritize coherence over correctness. While they are trained to generate text that sounds plausible, they lack a true understanding of facts and cannot reliably distinguish between verified information and fictional extrapolation. In high-stakes fields like mathematics, medicine, and law, where precision is paramount, such hallucinations can lead to serious misinformation and even real-world consequences.[65] Perhaps a new generation of LLMs (or other model) will find a better balance between coherence and correctness.

In addition, technologies cannot fix human fallacies —they might even reinforce and amplify them. Social media platforms have introduced AI tools that could, in theory, help people fact-check and create a better information environment. Yet these functions remain rarely used. The reasons are clear:[66]

- **Information overload**
  The sheer volume of content makes fact-checking overwhelming.

- **Speed of misinformation**
  False claims spread faster than corrections can catch up and can pay dividends for bad actors that want to affect public opinion, sway elections, or just sow discontent.

- **Trust in sources**
  People tend to believe information that aligns with their existing views and values.

- **Lack of incentive**
  There's little personal reward for verifying facts but plenty for sharing engaging content.

- **AI limitations**
  Automated fact-checking is imperfect and can generate misleading responses. More fundamentally, AI doesn't 'know' what it's doing—it operates statistically, not epistemically. It doesn't possess understanding, intent, or a sense of truth. And when it gets things wrong, there's no internal alarm, no error signal rooted in experience or instinct. But perhaps more worryingly, humans often don't react viscerally to falsehoods either. Simply, being wrong doesn't trigger nausea or a bloody nose. We lack a built-in 'truth nerve.' As long as the answer sounds confident and plausible, we often nod along. This creates a perfect storm: machines that confidently hallucinate, and humans who comfortably absorb it.
  > **Platform dynamics**: Social media companies prioritize engagement over accuracy.
  > **Echo chambers**: Users mostly interact with like-minded people, reinforcing biases.
  > **Technological constraints**: Even with AI, real-time misinformation detection remains a challenge.

Ultimately, social media thrives on engagement, not accuracy. Users often share content that resonates emotionally rather than verifying its truthfulness.

The problem isn't just technological—it's human behavior. Without a shift toward valuing accuracy over virality, misinformation will continue to thrive.

Yet another misconception is that AI will inherently lead to greater equality and democratization. While it has the potential to expand access to information and enhance productivity, its benefits are not evenly distributed. AI often amplifies the output of those already highly skilled or well resourced, widening the gap between the 'best and the rest.'[67] High performers see exponential gains, while those without access to top-tier tools or training risk being left behind. Without deliberate intervention—through policy, education, and equitable AI deployment—technology could exacerbate inequality rather than reduce it.

CHAPTER FOUR: WILL WE LET AI CHANGE US?

THE ALTAVISTA TRAP

In the mid-1990s, AltaVista was the dominant search engine, offering speed and comprehensive web indexing far ahead of its time. Launched in 1995 by Digital Equipment Corporation, it was a technological marvel, handling millions of searches daily. But despite this early lead, AltaVista failed to maintain its dominance. It wasn't ignorance of change that doomed it—it was an inability to adapt.[68]

AltaVista's downfall is a textbook case of what management scholar Don Sull calls active inertia[69]—the tendency of successful organizations to stick to old habits, even when the environment shifts. The company saw the rise of Google, but instead of doubling down on search, it tried to transform into a web portal, chasing Yahoo's model. This decision diluted its core function and frustrated users. By the time AltaVista attempted to pivot back to search, it was too late. Google had already redefined the game with a better algorithm and a cleaner, more focused interface.[70]

The same forces that trapped AltaVista now stand in the way of AI adoption in large organizations. AI has the potential to reshape industries by automating complex tasks, improving decision-making, and creating new business models. But most companies are too entangled in their existing systems, workflows, and habits to change direction. Instead of embracing AI-driven shifts, they tweak the old ways of doing things, making real transformation even harder.

Regulations often reinforce this inertia by protecting incumbents from disruption. Banking capital requirements make it difficult for fintech startups to challenge traditional banks. Tariffs on Chinese electric cars in Europe and the US shield legacy automakers from more competitive alternatives. Taxi licensing laws resisted ride sharing platforms for years, and occupational licensing in law and medicine limits competition from AI-driven services. Even copyright extensions, pushed by media giants, slow down technological shifts in entertainment and publishing. The result? The status quo lingers far longer than it should, even when better alternatives exist.

Take industries like finance, healthcare, and manufacturing—AI could improve efficiency, predict trends, and personalize services. But adopting it isn't just about adding new tools. It requires companies to rethink how they operate, retrain employees for new roles, and experiment with different ways of working. Without this effort, they risk ending up like AltaVista—outpaced by those that are willing to adapt.

Most companies don't fail because they don't see change coming. They fail because they have too much invested in the old system to climb down from one peak and scale a new one. The real winners of the AI era won't be those who merely incorporate AI into their existing structures—they'll be the ones willing to rebuild from the ground up.

WHY AI CAN'T TRANSFORM EDUCATION OVERNIGHT

If the technology is here and it works, why hasn't it transformed classrooms? Because education isn't just about learning—it's a deeply embedded system, a business, with rules, traditions, and constraints that resist rapid change and protect incumbents. Schools in Europe and the USA cannot change overnight because they are bound by legislation, bureaucracy, and deeply ingrained expectations. Policies take years to rewrite. Standardized testing, accreditation, and teacher certification are designed for stability, not rapid innovation. No politician wants to gamble an election on an untested education system. No parent wants their child to be an experiment. Schools also serve functions beyond learning—they provide childcare, structure, and social development. Shifting to AI-driven or even AI-assisted education would mean rethinking the role of teachers, retraining a workforce already in short supply, and redesigning school infrastructure.

This inertia is not unique to education. Automation has often struggled to replace human labor, even when it seems inevitable. Self-driving cars were supposed to eliminate Uber drivers, yet real-world complexity has kept humans in control. Factory robots have taken over repetitive tasks, but they require skilled technicians, making automation more expensive, not less. AI doesn't just replace—it reshapes work in ways that demand adaptation, new skills, and, often, higher costs.

Even if classrooms could transform, universities and employers still expect traditional credentials. If AI education teaches prompting, problem-solving, and creativity, but universities continue demanding standardized test scores, students will be caught in a mismatch between learning and assessment. The job market moves slowly, and without alignment, AI-driven education risks leaving students unprepared for outdated hiring systems.

The cost of full-scale AI integration into education would be staggering—likely in the trillions. Countries would need to invest in curriculum redesign, teacher retraining, infrastructure upgrades, and policy changes, all while ensuring that AI-driven learning doesn't deepen educational inequality. The wealthiest schools would adopt AI first, while underfunded districts would lag, creating an even wider gap.

AUSTIN'S LAW OF INSTITUTIONAL RESISTANCE

Technological change happens fast. Institutional change does not. Many industries today look almost identical to their pre-internet versions—courthouses still run on paper, churches still follow centuries-old traditions, and government offices still function like they did in the 20th century. AI may be powerful, but institutions are designed with checks and balances to resist disruption.

The so-called Austin's Law captures this resistance mathematically:

$$r = f(n^m)$$

where r is the internal resistance to new ideas, n is the number of employees, and m is the number of management levels, raised to an exponent. The larger the organization and the more layers of bureaucracy, the stronger the resistance.

Take military and defense, which in many ways should be one of the slowest-moving institutions. Large bureaucracies and long procurement cycles should slow top-down AI adoption. But on the ground, where survival is at stake, change happens fast. The use of civilian-built drones in Ukraine, after Russia's invasion, has shown that in wartime, technology leapfrogs bureaucracy and spreads organically. In wartime life-and-death situations, adoption speeds up dramatically.

Contrast this with healthcare and medicine, where patient safety regulations, legal liability, and deeply ingrained training pathways slow down AI adoption. AI can already diagnose diseases, analyze medical scans, and optimize hospital logistics, but rolling out these systems takes years. No one wants to be the first to trust an AI-driven doctor. Change will take decades, not years.

Banking and finance are similarly slow-moving due to regulations and risk aversion. While AI is already transforming fraud detection and algorithmic trading, more radical shifts—like decentralized finance or AI-driven banking—face significant government pushback. Stability matters more than speed, meaning that real change could take decades.

Law and judiciary operate on precedent. The legal system still relies on human judgment, paperwork, and courtroom procedures that have remained largely unchanged for centuries. AI could theoretically automate transcripts, legal research, contract drafting, and even case law analysis, but courts will continue to rely on court reporters, traditional lawyers, and judges. True transformation in the legal system could take decades.

Governments are among the slowest-moving entities when it comes to AI adoption. Bureaucracy, political cycles, and legacy systems make rapid change nearly impossible. AI could streamline public records and automate policymaking, but government structures resist automation for fear of disruption. In some cases, bureaucracies have actively fought against digital transformation. Meaningful AI adoption in public administration could take years.

Construction and urban planning could be revolutionized by AI-driven zoning, 3D-printed buildings, and automated smart cities. Yet outdated building codes, zoning laws, and government red tape keep the industry moving at a 20- to 40-year pace.

Finally, religious institutions represent the ultimate example of institutional resistance. These organizations are built around doctrine and tradition, and major shifts take centuries. AI may influence ethical debates, but fundamental religious structures will be among the last to change. Resistance to AI here isn't just about bureaucracy—it's about belief.

If AI adoption were driven purely by technological capability, it would already be everywhere. But institutions function on their own timelines, dictated by regulations, human behavior, and deeply embedded resistance. AI's future will arrive, but not all at once. It will unfold in waves, shaped less by the technology itself and more by the structures that must absorb it.

CONCLUSION: THE GRAVITY OF CHANGE

AI's arrival feels like a rupture—an inflection point where everything should shift. And yet, history warns us that transformation is never guaranteed.

The institutions that shape our world—schools, governments, banks, courts—have long resisted technological revolutions, and AI will be no different. Its potential is undeniable, but adoption will be shaped by inertia, missteps, and the weight of old habits. We like to believe that the best ideas rise to the top, that efficiency prevails, and that breakthroughs naturally replace the outdated. But history suggests otherwise. The wheel existed for centuries before it transformed transport. Electricity took decades to reshape industry. The internet, despite its ubiquity, has yet to truly rewire how most institutions function.

Take schools, for example, when the only time we seriously attempted an internet-first model was during the pandemic lockdowns of the early 2020s, and most found it disastrous. But that failure was not necessarily because of remote learning's inherent shortcomings

—it was proof of our failure to prepare. Instead of decades spent refining a digital education model, we rushed into it overnight trying to replicate analog classrooms in video conferences. Nobody came out of it sensing that a better school had been invented. It also exposed deep inequalities between the haves and have-nots—within families, where access to technology and parental support varied dramatically, and between nations, where wealthier countries adapted, while poorer ones saw entire generations fall behind. Technology alone cannot fix human fallacies and societal failures.

We can easily see how the same mistake will be repeated with AI. Its early missteps and overhyped promises will tempt many to dismiss it. Nothing kills opportunity—in organizations and societies—like, "We have tried that before, and it didn't work." Every transformative technology begins as an imperfect prototype. The first automobiles stalled more than they ran, the first airplanes crashed, and the first computers seemed too impractical for widespread use. If history teaches us anything, it is that the most significant breakthroughs don't arrive fully formed. They demand persistence.

The real question is not what AI can do but what we are willing to do with it and what we are willing to dismantle because of it. Will we use it merely to patch the cracks in our institutions, or will we reimagine what is possible? Will we allow its early flaws to become an excuse for clinging to the past, or will we push through the discomfort of reinvention?

One thing is certain: technology does not wait for permission. It moves with or without us. And those who resist it risk being left behind.

PART 3

GROW!

Societies face a defining moment. AI is no longer just an experiment—it is being integrated into the foundations of institutions, industries, and governance. But will it be used to reinforce the status quo, destabilize existing systems, or transform them for the better?

We have outlined four potential paths forward: Disruption, Departure, Diffusion, and Demonstration. Now, we must decide: Do we patch existing structures to accommodate AI, or do we pave entirely new roads?

This chapter explores how AI can be made useful—not just in the abstract but as a practical tool for economic growth, social cohesion, and institutional renewal. How do democratic societies integrate AI in a way that is both effective and aligned with their values? What is the best route for the USA, Europe, and other democracies?

CHAPTER FIVE

PATCHING IN THE TACTICAL PHASE

THE MUDDY ROAD AHEAD

In 1888, there were no petrol stations, so Bertha Benz had to rely on a local chemist in Wiesloch—a small town just south of Mannheim, barely visible on Google Maps unless you zoom all the way in. Petrol, as we know it, didn't exist either. Instead, Benz purchased ligroin, a solvent used by the Benz Patent-Motorwagen as fuel. This single-cylinder, three-wheeled vehicle, invented by her husband Karl Benz, is widely regarded as the world's first automobile.

Karl Benz's journey to this point had been anything but smooth. He had spent decades wrestling with business failures—many rescued by his wife's dowry—before finally assembling his key patents: the two-stroke engine, spark plug, carburetor, and radiator. These components, brought together through his experiments with engines and a bicycle repair shop in Mannheim, gave birth to the 'horseless carriage.'

But the real breakthrough wasn't the invention itself—it was Bertha's 100-kilometer journey to visit her mother in Pforzheim. The trip was an unglamorous trial by fire. The car broke down repeatedly, forcing Bertha to improvise repairs along the way. Hills presented a near-impossible challenge, revealing a critical flaw that would later inspire the addition of a third gear. Her insights, born of necessity, drove meaningful improvements that helped transform Karl's invention into something practical. Today, her historic trip is commemorated in Germany with a biannual antique automobile race along the same route.

Bertha Benz's story reminds us that new technology never evolves in a vacuum. It must be road-tested, exposing its flaws and forcing it to adapt to real-world conditions. Only through this messy, iterative process can it address shortcomings and meet societal needs. Moreover, testing out a new technology is a leap of faith that requires courage.

Bertha Benz's historic journey reminds us that new technologies are only as good as the environments they enter. The automobile wasn't ready for the world, and the world wasn't ready for the automobile—until both evolved together. AI is facing a similar reality. While its creators envision a world where machines enhance human intelligence and automate complex tasks, the reality is messier. AI was built for a frictionless, digital-first world, but it's being thrust into systems that were never designed for autonomous decision-making, machine-generated content, or large-scale automation. Just as early automobiles struggled on roads meant for horses and carts, AI is struggling in an ecosystem that wasn't designed for it. To reiterate one of this book's themes, tools don't change the world, but mindsets do.

This chapter explores the practical, often unglamorous phase of AI adoption—what we call patching.

AI is already here, but many of our institutions aren't ready for it. The first phase of adaptation is not about grand reinvention—it's about duct tape. History has shown us that every transformative technology—whether automobiles, the internet, or AI—begins as an ambitious vision but soon collides with reality. When the world wasn't ready for the automobile, roads had to change. When the world wasn't ready for the internet, rules had to be rewritten. Why should we expect the world to be ready for the transformative potential of AI-enabled systems? How can we more effectively use duct tape as we learn about the limits of technology? How can we improve system designs faster so less tape is needed to achieve a desired effect?

FLAWED VISIONS

Few publications were as eclectic as the Whole Earth Catalog. Born in the late 1960s on the West Coast of the United States, it embodied the hippie ideals of self-sufficiency, ecology, alternative education, 'do it yourself' (DIY), and holism. Its pages were part mail-order catalog of eccentric, sometimes useful gadgets, and part collection of essays on ecology and the future. The catalog has since been dubbed the "internet before the internet."[71]

When we reflect on the early days of the World Wide Web, the hippie influence is unmistakable: an open world without borders, where everything—information, music, movies, and more—was free to share. Yet while living in a hippie commune might offer spiritual benefits, it's not for everyone. There's a reason Burning Man, the desert festival rooted in countercultural ideals, lasts only a week. Similarly, the first decades of widespread internet adoption have been about patching up the potholes left by its countercultural origins. Payment systems, ownership templates, identity verification tools, and cybersecurity shields have transformed the free-for-all commune into a less idealistic but more functional capitalist city.

Artificial intelligence was similarly born as an ideal—an aspiration to program computers to think and behave like humans. This ambition aligns with the Ayn Rand-inspired ethos of Silicon Valley, where disruptive technologies are celebrated for outpacing slower, less capable systems, whether those systems are traditional companies or human cognitive processes.

However, this 'might-makes-right' mentality has given rise to numerous systemic issues and unintended consequences:[72]

- **Data Theft at Scale**
  Training massive AI models requires enormous datasets often obtained without consent, blurring the line between innovation and intellectual property theft. A prime example is the lawsuit against OpenAI and Meta, where authors and artists have accused these companies of scraping their copyrighted works without permission to train their models.[73] It was ironic that OpenAI would later accuse China's DeepSeek and Manus chatbots for having "inappropriately" copied ChatGPT.[74] In the land-grab that is AI development, anything goes, it seems.

- **Environmental Strain**
  The rapid growth of AI imposes significant environmental costs. While the human brain operates on roughly 20 watts—less than a dim light bulb—AI systems consume gigawatts of electricity annually, straining power grids during a global climate crisis.

Data centers, critical for AI operations, also deplete freshwater supplies for cooling at unsustainable rates, exacerbating water scarcity in vulnerable regions. Moreover, sprawling data centers encroach on green spaces and farmland. A recent study found that each month ChatGPT use is producing the same amount of CO_2 emissions as 260 flights from New York City to London, underscoring the hidden costs of widespread AI adoption.[75]

- **Unreliable Output**
  AI systems frequently generate 'hallucinations,' producing incorrect or misleading information with high confidence. These errors arise from limitations in training data, model architecture, and the probabilistic nature of AI responses.[76] Bias further compounds the problem, as models can reinforce and amplify existing prejudices. This makes AI an inherently unpredictable tool—not yet reliable enough for systems that demand a very low or zero tolerance for failure, such as the judicial system, where accuracy and fairness are paramount. Addressing these challenges requires ongoing improvements in training methods, transparency, and human oversight.

- **Digital Pollution**
  Not only is technology unable to fix human fallacies—it can amplify and facilitate our worst instincts, from deception and exploitation to greed and manipulation.
  AI-generated spam is increasingly inundating social media platforms, with reports highlighting a surge in low-quality, AI-produced content cluttering users' feeds. This proliferation of 'AI slop' not only

degrades user experience but also makes it harder to distinguish genuine content from fabricated material.[77] Concurrently, the rise of non-consensual deepfake pornography has inflicted significant harm, predominantly targeting women. Studies indicate that a vast majority of deepfake videos online are pornographic, with 99% of the victims being women.[78] These malicious creations lead to severe emotional distress, reputational damage, and violations of privacy. The deluge of AI-generated content and the misuse of deepfake technology threaten to undermine the credibility and safety of digital spaces, necessitating robust measures to combat these challenges.

- **Software Degradation**
The initial integration of AI into established software platforms has, in some cases, led to a decline in user experience. For instance, Google's rollout of AI-powered overviews in search results, known as Search Generative Experiences, faced significant criticism upon its release. Users reported inaccuracies and irrelevant information, leading to frustration and a surge in searches on how to disable the feature. This negative reception highlights the challenges of implementing AI without compromising the quality and reliability that users expect.[79] Similarly, Adobe's introduction of AI features in its Creative Cloud suite has been met with mixed reactions. While some users appreciate the innovative tools, others express concerns that the focus on AI detracts from core functionalities, leading to a degraded user experience. This sentiment is evident in discussions where users question the prioritization of AI over

resolving existing software issues.[80] These examples underscore a critical point: first impressions of AI integration are pivotal. If users' initial experiences are negative, it becomes challenging to build trust and encourage widespread adoption of new technologies like the type AI enables. Ensuring that AI enhancements genuinely add value without undermining existing functionalities is essential for fostering user confidence and acceptance.

- **Catastrophic Forgetting and the Opaque Nature of AI**
  As AI systems evolve, they face an inherent challenge known as catastrophic forgetting—a phenomenon where a model loses previously acquired knowledge as it learns new information. This issue arises due to the model's inability to retain old data while incorporating new updates, potentially leading to inconsistencies and degraded performance over time. Addressing catastrophic forgetting is crucial to ensuring that AI remains a reliable and consistent tool, especially in applications requiring long-term accuracy.[81] This problem is compounded by the inherent opacity of LLMs—even their developers do not fully understand how they process and store information. Unlike traditional software systems, where every function can be explicitly traced and debugged, LLMs operate as black boxes, with complex neural pathways adjusting dynamically based on new inputs. This lack of transparency makes it difficult to predict when or why a model might 'forget' crucial information. Researchers continue to explore ways to make LLMs more interpretable and reliable, but significant challenges remain.[82]

- **Accuracy Decay**

  AI models don't just make mistakes—they often become less reliable over time. A recent study[83] found that GPT-4's performance on certain tasks, such as solving math problems and identifying false statements, has significantly declined since its launch. This phenomenon, sometimes referred to as 'model drift,' occurs because AI systems are continuously updated with new data and optimizations that can inadvertently degrade some prior capabilities. The causes remain unclear, as even AI developers struggle to pinpoint why performance fluctuates. Unlike traditional software, where bugs can be fixed systematically, LLMs operate in ways that make regression difficult to diagnose and prevent. As AI becomes increasingly embedded in critical applications—from legal analysis to medical diagnosis—its tendency to degrade unpredictably presents serious challenges. Without rigorous benchmarking, transparent auditing, and more stable update mechanisms, AI systems may become 'too' unreliable precisely when users need them most.

Just as the invention of the ship simultaneously led to the invention of the shipwreck, we are navigating AI's unpredictable and often hazardous journey. Many of the issues outlined above—data theft, environmental strain, unreliable outputs, digital pollution, software degradation, and catastrophic forgetting—stem from a fundamental tension: AI has been thrust into systems that were never designed for it. These failures aren't just inconvenient; they erode trust in AI and AI-enabled systems at a time when fears of job displacement and its widening inequality are shaping public perception. Instead of smoothing the transition, these problems risk reinforcing skepticism, making it even harder to realize AI's potential in ways that best serve society.

Yet AI is evolving rapidly, and its limitations are not set in stone. As AI researcher and author Ethan Mollick reminds us: "Assume this is the worst AI you will ever use. We are playing Pac-Man in a world that will soon have PlayStation 6."[84] AI will improve—its outputs will become more accurate, its environmental footprint more efficient, and its integration into daily life more seamless. But in today's hyper competitive world, waiting for that future is not an option. Institutions, businesses, and individuals must learn how to leverage and work with AI as it is today, flaws and all.

This chapter explores the pragmatic phase of AI adoption—what we call 'patching.' AI is already here, but institutions weren't designed for it. This first adaptation stage is not grand reinvention—it's duct tape, short-term, messy, and inelegant solutions. Just as the internet evolved from an open, chaotic experiment into a structured system—shaped by market forces, user demand, business innovation, and governance—AI is now being hastily integrated into existing frameworks. Patching is a tactical, low-risk way to test AI's utility before committing to large-scale change. It's about iterating, experimenting, and protecting institutions from making irreversible, costly mistakes. It works bottom-up, just like electricity once did.

BACK TO THE FUTURE

New technology often mimics old structures before finding its proper form. The first automobiles looked like horseless carriages. The first personal computers, dubbed 'word processors,' were just glorified typewriters. When modern aviation emerged after World War II, it borrowed heavily from maritime traditions—a 'captain' with striped sleeves, ship 'stewards,' 'aft' and 'port' side, 'cruising' altitude, and so on. Institutions tend to force new technology into familiar workflows rather than rethinking processes from the ground up.

The first three chapters in this book show how individuals and companies use AI in much the same way: as patches rather than revolutions. A personal assistant, a spell checker on steroids—or was it LSD?—and an ideation tool. AI today isn't replacing industries; it's enhancing specific tasks where risks are manageable, costs are low, and the upside is big.

This is a familiar pattern. In the introduction, we visited the New York Electrical Show of 1919 and saw the speculative prototypes that teased the gadgets electricity would bring into households. Because there was no electric grid, homes adopted electricity in isolated ways—electric sewing machines, standalone electric fans, and electric irons replacing coal-heated ones. Redundant, yes, but necessary stepping stones. At the time, it was even predicted that "it will be extremely difficult to find any farm home ... which will not be equipped with a [...] power plant of some kind."[85]

AI is advancing through incremental patches—small, low-risk improvements with outsized benefits. Instead of sweeping disruptions, its most effective applications fine-tune, accelerate, and enhance existing processes. These tactical wins stack up, creating momentum without demanding wholesale reinvention.

But where has AI already proven its utility—not just for the best and brightest, but for everyone? And what can this tell us about which areas are ripe for rapid adaptation, where institutions can seamlessly integrate AI to unlock immediate value?

Where is AI already making people better at what they do—not through grand upheavals, but through practical, measurable enhancements that compound over time?

AI'S EQUALIZERS AND AMPLIFIERS

AI adoption today is fragmented. Individuals experiment with chatbots and generative tools, companies implement selective solutions, and nations are yet to develop large-scale AI infrastructure is akin to the broadband expansion of the late 1990s. For now, AI remains an imperfect patchwork layered onto existing systems, offering immediate tactical advantages.

So where does AI deliver the most value? We can categorize its impact into two key functions:

- **Equalizers**
  AI tools that level the playing field by enabling less skilled workers to perform at a higher level.

- **Amplifiers**
  AI tools that give top performers an edge, allowing them to push boundaries even further.

EQUALIZERS: RAISING THE FLOOR

Coding Efficiency
AI significantly boosts productivity, especially for less experienced developers. Studies show that developers using GitHub Copilot completed tasks 55.8% faster.[86] A broader study across major firms found AI-assisted developers completed 26% more tasks, with junior developers seeing up to a 40% boost.[87]

Customer Services
Generative AI in support roles led to a 15% increase in productivity, with newer employees improving by 30%, reducing skill gaps and improving customer interactions.[88]

Writing & Copywriting
AI-assisted professionals complete tasks 40% faster with an 18% improvement in quality.[89] Non-experts benefit most when using AI as a 'sounding board' rather than a 'ghostwriter,' enhancing ad copy performance.[90]

Legal Work
AI aids legal analysis, especially for less-experienced users, improving efficiency by 12% to 32%.[91] While quality gains are inconsistent, AI reduces performance disparities, benefiting those with lower baseline skills.

AMPLIFIERS: PUSHING THE CEILING

While AI can act as an equalizer, enhancing productivity for lower-skilled individuals, it can also serve as an amplifier, disproportionately benefiting those already excelling in their fields.

Entrepreneurship
A study on Kenyan entrepreneurs found that AI mentorship provided significant benefits—but only to those already excelling. High-performing entrepreneurs saw a 15% increase in performance, while lower performers experienced an 8% decline.[92] This suggests that AI assistance in business settings may not be a universal accelerator but rather an enhancer for those who can already navigate complex decisions effectively.

Debating
A university study on AI-assisted debating found that while AI use led to a 9.2% increase in debate success, the benefits were concentrated among high-ability students. Scholarship recipients improved by 12%, while lower-performing students saw little to no benefit.[93] This suggests that AI may amplify pre-existing cognitive advantages in skill-based competitions.

Investing
AI's impact on financial decision-making also favors those with expertise. Investors using AI-generated summaries that matched their level of financial sophistication improved their decision-making, while those receiving mismatched assistance performed worse.[94]

This underscores the importance of AI alignment with user expertise—otherwise, it risks widening gaps rather than closing them.

PLAYING AROUND IN THE SANDBOX PHASE

With AI, we are all like Bertha Benz. We are hopping into and onto a new technological marvel with the future largely charted by decisions from this point forward. Some have to hide it for their employer while others are free—even encouraged—to experiment and choose for themselves how to leverage its capabilities. AI isn't replacing industries just yet but enhancing specific tasks that users see value in, and because legacy systems at first absorb new technologies—rather than vice versa—AI is strongest where it acts as an assistant to human capabilities, not as a replacement for human capabilities.

In this playful phase, however, things can be done on an enterprise level to prepare for the transformational changes AI will bring. The Transforming Transportation Advisory Committee (I served on as the Vice-chair of the AI sub committee) suggested to the US Department of Transportation[95] four areas of recommendations that I believe apply to government, industry, and other organizations: (1) prepare for AI,

(2) foster a trustworthy culture for AI, (3) realize the benefits of AI, and (4) manage the risks of AI.

A crucial element of this sandbox phase is about building the right understanding: knowing what AI models can and cannot do. As Eric Schmidt said in a 2024 interview at Stanford, "The best-case scenario is that you know what your model is capable of." That's not a given—and therein lies both opportunity and danger. AI's development vividly illustrates Moravec's paradox:[96] models can often perform complex, abstract tasks surprisingly well, yet fail at tasks humans consider simple and intuitive. This cognitive mismatch can lead us to overtrust or misapply AI systems. Aligning our mental model of AI's capabilities with the actual state of the technology is key—otherwise, we risk giving it responsibility that it cannot yet (or should not) bear.

The Spinoff: When the airline industry was deregulated in the 1990s, incumbent flag carriers were challenged by low-cost, no-frills alternatives (like Southwest Airlines in the USA and Ryanair in Europe). What many airlines then did—after having at first sneered and disregarded the new competitors—was to create spinoffs, like Qantas's Jetstar or Singapore Airlines' Scoot, that could offer an alternative without tainting the mother brand and limiting potential downsides if the experiment failed. It was a kind of toe-dip strategy rather than a 180-degree strategy. Experimentation is a misunderstood word. Most think it entails scientists doing random things with a range of variables to see what works in proving a hypothesis. In reality, in business and policy, it can be a way to test the water and fail sustainably. It's not an experiment if you blow up the lab or sink the whole ship. With AI, a law firm could create a low-cost, fully automated legal service on the side to open up for new kinds of customers.

The Freemium Buffet: When online shopping was new, brick-and-mortar stores were seen as places to experience the brand, while online was dismissed as glorified mail order. A similar divide exists with AI today —many still prefer human interaction over automation. This creates an opportunity: businesses can offer a tiered experience, where AI handles basic tasks for free or at a lower cost, while premium human-assisted services remain available for those who value them.

Airlines already do this with self check-in versus staffed counters (often provided for free only to their most loyal customers). A law firm might offer automated contract reviews for free but charge for expert consultation. The key is flexibility—letting customers choose their preferred mix of AI and human service rather than forcing a one-size-fits-all approach.

The Trojan Horse: In the early days of personal computing, software like Lotus 1-2-3 and later Microsoft Excel were quietly introduced into enterprises as productivity boosters, often without formal IT approval. AI can follow a similar path. Instead of mandating full AI integration across an organization, companies can deploy AI in an unobtrusive way—packaging it within existing workflows. For example, AI-powered summarization tools can be embedded into email clients, or meeting assistants can be introduced as simple note-takers before evolving into decision-support systems. Much like spreadsheets, IT, HR, and others remain on the catch-up working to guide employees on the best utilization of these new tools.

The Parallel Play: Children often engage in 'parallel play' before learning to cooperate. Similarly, AI and human professionals can work alongside each other in loosely integrated ways before deeper collaboration takes hold. Instead of forcing AI into roles that replace human expertise, organizations can allow employees to shadow AI—using it as a real-time benchmarking tool to compare insights. For instance, a financial firm might let human analysts make investment decisions but require them to cross-check AI-generated risk assessments before proceeding.

The Co-Pilot Strategy: The road to fully autonomous vehicles isn't a sudden leap but a gradual evolution. Cars have long had assistive technologies—starting with cruise control in the 1950s, then evolving to adaptive cruise control, lane-keeping assistance, automated parking, assistive driving, and in select instances highly automated driving. Today's AI-powered driving assistants represent an intermediate step where human drivers remain in control, but AI handles specific tasks, reducing fatigue, improving safety, and enhancing the quality and quantity of outcomes.

The White Label Model: Companies can embed AI into services without advertising it, like store-brand products made by premium manufacturers. A travel agency might use AI for itineraries while presenting them as handcrafted. But if AI's role is discovered—especially after an error—it can erode trust. Today, transparency and human oversight help mitigate this risk.

The Fire Escape Plan: Every innovation comes with risks, and organizations could establish an AI 'fire escape plan.' This means defining clear criteria for when an AI implementation should be scaled back or reworked. What are the red flags? What is the point of no return? Just as well-managed startups set guardrails for burn rate and pivoting, companies experimenting with AI should consider the value of establishing predefined exit strategies to avoid costly mistakes.

The Phased Handoff: Rather than replacing human workers overnight, AI can be introduced in phases, gradually shifting responsibility over time. Consider how plug-in hybrid electric vehicles eased consumers toward fully electric vehicles. Similarly, AI can start by assisting workers in simple tasks, later taking over more complex roles as confidence and trust build. For example, AI in customer services can begin by answering FAQs before gradually handling more nuanced inquiries.

THE RELEVANCE PROBLEM

In the early 2020s, a diamond was no longer forever. The icy rocks created by carbon compressed over a million years had been rivalled, even replaced, by synthetic diamonds, made in a lab over a couple of weeks. The retail price was about 80% less than the natural alternative. The diamonds look the same and are built from the same raw material, so what do you do if you are a jewelry store or a diamond miner? How do you stay relevant in a world that is constantly moving? How will consumers choose between natural and synthetic?

The diamond industry is part of a long list of challenged incumbents, from 80s hair metal bands that were obsolete when grunge entered the music scene in the early 1990s to the Nokias and Kodaks of the world. There is no easy answer or silver bullet to how to stay relevant, but there are a few learnings to bear in mind as AI challenges the status quo:

Success is toxic

These are the words from Nokia's former chairman Risto Siilasmaa when he explained why Nokia's 40% market share in mobile phones vanished in the phase of Apple and Android smartphones. A successful company tends to be arrogant, lazy, and slow.

Speaking about Apple, the Cupertino-based behemoth has famously missed out on building an AI-driven iOS. They made two significant bets: that AI capability growth would be slower than anticipated and that users would care about on-device piracy. The latter successfully created iTunes, where people could legally buy MP3 music in a time of illegal file sharing services, like Napster and Kazaa. Both bets, however, turned out to be wrong about AI. As technology analyst Mark Gurman puts it:

> Apple Inc., the company behind the Mac, iPhone, iPad and other groundbreaking products, has typically beaten rivals by following the hockey approach: skate to where the puck is going to be, rather than where it is right now. But we're currently in the middle of the biggest technology revolution since the debut of the internet, and Apple is barely even on the ice.

Yesterday's winner is rarely—if ever—tomorrow's dominant player. Success is toxic.

Be radically curious about new competitors

Companies tend to cultivate pride, but this can easily translate to arrogance, especially if new challengers enter the scene. Instead of trying to understand what the market thinks of the new entrant—ultimately the only opinion that matters in business—companies sneer, ignore, and deny.

Accept that large companies are not built for change
The fable told about Blockbuster Video is one of technological disruption—as video cassettes and DVDs were replaced by online alternatives. The reality, as explained by Alan Payne,[97] one of Blockbuster's largest franchisees back in the 1990s, was that the company was never built to change, only to grow. The founder, Wayne Huizenga, had practiced the consolidation model when he built Waste Management. Garbage trucks were small and local, so he bought up trucks and routes, created a cohesive brand and color scheme, and enabled behind-the-scenes synergy, like cost sharing and procurement. Before Blockbuster, video stores were small and local, so Huizenga did the same thing; he bought them up and created a cohesive brand and color scheme and enabled behind-the-scenes synergy, like cost sharing and procurement. Blockbuster was built to grow, not to change. The title of Alan Payne's book about the rise and fall of the company says it all—*Built to Fail*.

What You Think You're Selling vs. What People Are Buying
The market decides 'why' you matter. The Swiss watch industry once believed it was selling precision timekeeping—until the quartz revolution made it clear that digital watches were cheaper and more accurate. What endured wasn't the utility of timekeeping but the intangible value: craftsmanship, heritage, status. That's why Rolex thrived while others collapsed. Similarly, Hollywood thought it was selling cinema—until TikTok, YouTube, and streaming showed that audiences were also hungry

for distraction, novelty, and quick emotional payoffs. The core product didn't disappear, but the reason people consumed it evolved. AI will force similar reckonings. If algorithms can generate music, art, or legal documents, the value of 'human-made versions' must lie elsewhere: authenticity, taste, context, connection, or brand. The companies that survive won't just defend their outputs—they'll reframe their value in terms the market actually cares about.

Attack the future
Companies cannot commit suicide. No board of directors will willingly kill off its core business, even when disruption is inevitable. Instead, they defend, delay, and deny—fighting to preserve what once made them successful rather than building what will keep them relevant. Taxi companies lobbied against Uber instead of reinventing ride-hailing themselves. The music industry tried to crush Napster instead of creating Spotify. Today, German automakers cling to their century-old engineering prestige, while Chinese EV makers flood the market with cheaper, faster-moving alternatives. AI isn't a threat to business. Yet. But failing to experiment with AI is.

CONCLUSION: CHATBOT, THEN WHAT?

Patching is the first survival instinct of any system faced with disruption. It's the quick fix, the temporary bridge, the makeshift adaptation that allows industries to function without fully reinventing themselves. AI is no different. Companies are layering it onto existing processes, workers are using it to accelerate tedious tasks, and institutions are cautiously experimenting while trying to maintain control. This phase is tactical, messy, and imperfect—but necessary. AI today is where automobiles were when they still shared roads with horse-drawn carriages, where the internet was when it was a Wild West of piracy, pop-ups, and unstructured chaos.

But at some point, patching isn't enough. The automobile needed highways and gas stations. The internet needed payment systems and business models. AI will need new infrastructure—not just software tweaks and regulatory Band-Aids, but deep structural shifts in how industries, economies, and governments operate. One early example is the UK's approach to autonomous vehicle legislation.[98] Rather than simply retrofitting existing traffic laws, the Law Commission undertook a ground-up review, asking what legal and institutional frameworks would be needed if AI were a driver, not just a tool. This included rethinking liability, redefining agency, and even assigning responsibility to a new legal entity: the 'authorized self-driving entity.' In essence, they laid a new legal pavement rather than patching potholes in the old road.

Other examples could include:
- **Healthcare**: Moving from diagnosis-as-an-event to continuous, AI-monitored health baselines would require new insurance models, data-sharing regulations, and even medical training paradigms.
- **Education**: If AI tutors become widely effective, it challenges the basic economic model of schooling (teacher–student ratios, class sizes, curriculums) and forces a rethink of accreditation and assessment.

Each of these is less about slotting AI into existing workflows and more about designing workflows around what AI makes possible or problematic.

Right now, AI development is stuck in a myopic feedback loop, obsessing over slightly different versions of LLMs, each optimized for a slightly different 'vibe.' It's like an episode of *America's Next Top Model*, where companies are endlessly tweaking and styling their chatbots—who's the smartest, the most helpful, the most aligned?—without stopping to ask: How are these tools best poised to help businesses, consumers, or society? Can revenue offset the capital and operational costs? Venture firm Sequoia framed the current moment as the '$600B question'[99] and asked whether AI products can generate enough real-world value to justify their staggering compute and development costs.

The real challenge isn't making a chatbot that sounds more helpful or aligns slightly better with human preferences. The challenge is moving AI from engagement-driven gimmick to real-world utility. The first phase of the internet was flooded with websites optimized for clicks, much like today's AI is optimized for plausible-sounding responses. That worked for a while, but real business value emerged only when companies stopped chasing attention and started building lasting infrastructure—secure payments, identity verification, and cloud storage. AI will go through the same evolution, but only if companies shift focus from chasing engagement metrics to solving problems that fulfill user needs.

So what does that look like? It won't be as simple as adding AI to existing workflows. Some industries will need to rethink their entire operational structure. Others will need entirely new business or regulatory models. Countries will diverge in AI adoption, just as they did with industrialization, electricity, and the internet. Some will move fast and break things. Others will cautiously regulate before scaling. There are lessons to learn from history, as we'll see in the coming chapter—Henry Ford's horizontal factory, the internet's messy evolution, and the hidden economic forces that determine whether a new technology takes root or fades into irrelevance. AI's impact won't be measured in quarterly profits but in deeper, more structural shifts that will take decades.

The next phase of this book explores what happens after patching—when companies, industries, and nations start building the infrastructure for an AI-enabled economy, not just reacting to it.

The truth is, we don't really know how to measure the success of AI systems yet. 'Tasks automated' or 'costs saved' are blunt tools that mostly describe how we use AI to patch existing workflows. But the deeper value—like decision precision, resilience, or entirely new product classes—is still hard to quantify. In that sense, AI today is like electricity in 1900: everyone knows it's powerful, but no one has the accounting language to capture what it actually does.

Where will AI accelerate industries, and where will it stall? What are the real economic levers that determine its impact? And how do we avoid falling into the trap of optimizing AI for superficial engagement instead of long-term societal value?

We are at the crossroads between quick fixes and real transformation. Chatbots are just the beginning. The real question is: Then what?

CHAPTER SIX

PAVING IN THE STRATEGIC PHASE

FADING INTO THE FABRIC

Brevik tram station in suburban Stockholm is nobody's idea of an exciting place. It has two tracks, surrounded by apartment buildings and a grocery store. One track leads to the city, usually full of commuters in the morning; the other brings them back in the early evening. On a drab December day in late 2024, the platform is empty. But something has quietly changed. Two metal poles with blue boxes have been installed, and if you take the tram, you'll notice that all the human ticket inspectors have perished. Suburban Stockholm has belatedly embraced tap-your-phone, ticketless travel.

Now, imagine if someone had told you, back in the mid-1990s when the internet was new, that one day you would use your phone to tap on a box to buy a tram ticket. At the time, the telephone was still fixed in your kitchen, and the internet was a noisy modem tethered to your work PC. Hitting an object with your phone was something you might do out of frustration—not to make a purchase. The long-term future of new technology is often unimaginable in its early days. More importantly, optimizing the utility of a new technology requires us to go beyond patching and improvisation. It demands that we start paving the roads ahead, transforming infrastructure to embed the technology into the fabric of daily life—like the blue boxes on tram platforms in Stockholm. The question is whether we still can.

Once upon a time, we were able to do big things fast. The Empire State Building was conceived and finished within two years, The Eiffel Tower was built in two years and two months, the 1,700-mile Alaska Highway was finished in about half of that (234 days to be exact) and on August 9, 1968, NASA decided that Apollo 8 should go to the moon. It launched on December 21, 1968, a mere 134 days later.[100] Today, London Heathrow Airport has spent decades arguing about a third runway, and California's High Speed rail link has doubled in budget and halved its distance. It has been dubbed a "bullet train to nowhere" as the proposed trip between Los Angeles and San Francisco was scaled down to run between the less cosmopolitan Merced and Bakersfield.[101]

Alarmingly, when it comes to AI, IT projects are notorious when it comes to cost and timing overruns: nearly a fifth of them break the budget by more than 50%. And many sit unused on a shelf. Many countries have squandered billions on public IT projects only to have them scrapped after launch because of low usability. It seems almost like we're doomed to patch things forever. Something the cartoonist Randall Munroe picked up in his (in)famous cartoon about IT infrastructure.

Add to this list the difficulty of predicting the long-term usability of new technologies. The history of promising new technologies is rimmed by troughs of disillusionment. Airships is one example. Surely, they are the future. Less noisy and, more importantly, significantly less polluting than jet airplanes, we are likely to see the return of blimps. *The Economist* magazine thought so in 2024: "Airships may finally prove useful for transporting cargo," it proclaimed. In 2016, it had boldly predicted that "airships could be returning for commercial travel," while a 2014 article—under the aptly named section "Inflated Ideas"—heralded an age of "Reviving airships." The magazine has, in fact, predicted the return of airships several times over the past decades. It is just one example of a technology that, while interesting and useful, never takes off. The world is full of such examples, from nuclear energy powered by thorium, not uranium, to France's state-owned internet substitute, dubbed Minitel. Even electricity was mired in a battle for a standard between alternating current and direct current, with the former winning, while most modern devices like laptops run on direct current, which is why all charging cables have a clunky power adapter attached.

Gartner, a technology consultancy, famously plots technologies along a curve it calls the hype cycle, wherein something new is full of exciting potential. It climbs steadily along a curve of inflated expectation until it reaches its peak. Then it collapses into a trough of disillusionment where, as we see with airships or thorium, it can get stuck forever unless it manages a more steady, linear path to productivity.

Social media was once seen as a powerful force, not just to reconnect with high school buddies but also to generate social movements. When the Mubarak government of Egypt fell after mass protests in Cairo's Tahrir Square, part of the Arab Spring revolutions in the early 2010s, social media in general and Facebook, in particular, was credited as a liberation tool that transferred power from the tyrants to the people. It turned out to be the peak of inflated expectations. Only a few years later, after the Cambridge Analytica scandal exposed the vulnerability of Facebook feeds to propaganda, Facebook was credited with having destroyed elections. In 2024, Australia banned social media for under-16s, with more countries likely to follow. A force for freedom and friendship had been transformed into a sinister foe in less than a decade.

This chapter will outline how we can integrate AI into our world and build something larger, better, than what we have today. It will force us to move away from the corporate ventures and individual tools and start thinking about what kind of society we will want to live in, and what part AI will, and should, play in it. The first step is to realize that it takes time.

OPPORTUNITIES HIDDEN IN PLAIN SIGHT

History tells us that major technological shifts are rarely about individual breakthroughs. They require paving or at least stepping stones—rethinking infrastructure, institutions, and societal habits.

Take Murrays' Mills in Manchester, UK. These massive brick buildings, once the pride of the 19th-century industrial juggernaut, were built vertically because steam and coal were the dominant energy sources. The heavy boilers sat on the ground floor, with steam rising to power machines above. Urban land was expensive, so building upwards made economic sense, and factories were often located near waterways for transport.

Then, electricity arrived. But it took decades before pioneers like Henry Ford realized that electricity could be used for more than illumination. Ford saw that rather than moving workers to machines, as in steam-powered factories, goods could move along a conveyor belt, making automobile production vastly more efficient.

Just as it took time for the industrial world to transition from steam to electricity, AI's long-term success depends not on isolated tools but on systemic transformation. Are we capable of paving the road ahead?

NATIONAL PAVING STRATEGIES: MONEY OR FREEDOM?

Before 2015, the Golden Gate Bridge saw an average of 14 head-on collisions annually, resulting in two fatalities each year. That changed when authorities introduced a central barrier, reducing traffic deaths to zero. If such a simple solution can be so effective, why isn't a median barrier installed on every road in the USA? The primary reason is cost—it would be too expensive to implement nationwide.[102]

Now, take a moment to Google what Dubai used to look like in 1995. There are few, if any, skyscrapers, no world-class airport, no railways, no glitz or glamour. It resembles a drab suburb in the desert. In the decades since, Dubai's rise as one of the world's foremost tourist destinations and regional business hubs is remarkable.

Why can entire city states pop out of the desert wasteland in just a few decades when the USA cannot even put central barriers to prevent road deaths?

The difference comes down to two things: whether a country has access to money *or* freedom. Some countries lack either: Venezuela's chaotic autocracy comes to mind. Similarly, few have both money *and* freedom. Most countries are either freedom-rich but money-poor or money-rich but freedom-poor. Dubai is a benevolent autocracy with a technocratic and business-friendly approach. It combines absolute monarchy with elements of modern governance, strategic planning, and economic liberalism. This has enabled it to build big things fast.

Belgium, on the other hand, scores a nearly perfect 96 out of a 100 on the Freedom Index, an annual survey managed by the thinktank Freedom House[103] (the United Arab Emirates, of which Dubai is part, is at the other end of the spectrum with a paltry 18 out of a 100). While Belgium is in no way poor, it does not have access to the kind of capital needed to overhaul its infrastructure or build new business districts from scratch. Neither would it be able to since laws and politics are in place to prevent out-of-control public spending.

Dubai, China, and Saudi Arabia are examples of places that can rapidly change their cityscapes and institutions since they are not subject to the kind of checks-and-balances that most democracies are constitutionally bound to.

This means that in the short term, money-rich, freedom-poor countries—like China or some Gulf states—will have the opportunity to adapt to AI at a faster pace. For them, progress is primarily an engineering challenge: what to build, how to scale, and how fast. It's not about funding. This can seem seductive, especially to sluggish European economies, which are often freedom-rich but money-poor, hampered by layers of regulation and budgetary constraints. In these contexts, progress is a legalistic challenge—what can be done, with what resources, and under which timelines.

The USA occupies a third position: both money-rich and relatively freedom-rich, at least in terms of market-driven innovation. It benefits from the capital intensity of its tech sector and a more permissive regulatory environment, allowing it to experiment and commercialize AI at scale. But this also brings its own risks—when regulation lags too far behind deployment, the result can be societal backlash, capture by incumbents, or systemic misuse.

The slowness does have a vital function, however: we cannot know in advance exactly what will work and whether proposed changes undoubtedly lead to long-term improvement. If we want to find out whether a new drug works, we do clinical trials and record our findings extensively, rather than trusting a witch doctor shaman. Independent scientists and government agencies then scrutinize the findings and, if convinced, give the go-ahead for patient use. The result of this process has been miraculous in the past century. We have moved from the old world where alchemists cooked up whatever they felt like and sold it as an ointment, with longevity statistics staying flat or declining to a new world where life expectancy has risen dramatically thanks to better health and medication. This was not known in advance, and progress has been enabled by one cumbersome invention at a time, petri dish by petri dish. Experimentation is the art of failing sustainably. If the patient dies or we blow up the country, it is foolishness, not experimentation. An AI-powered school may have many advantages over its analogue counterparts, but if we are not sure of it, a complete overhaul of an education system risks leaving children worse off. And what parent in their right mind wants to use their child for potentially extremely high risk experimentation?

We may gaze admiringly at the glittering skylines of Shanghai and Dubai and frown at the seemingly stagnant European city centers. But we forget that European cities have burned down and been bombed several times.

They've had their populations decimated by the plague and all their workplaces vacated because of stock market crashes. Like steel, they have been hardened over time, to withstand a crisis and emerge stronger. The same goes for institutions. They are the accumulation of decades of collective wisdom, of wrong turns and dead ends as well as wise decisions and walkbacks. Like tree rings, they can inform us of a society's health over time and warn us about making the wrong decisions. They are dismantled at our peril.

This is why freedom-rich but money-poor countries will need to use acupunctural investing, instead: small experiments to see what works and where outcomes can be maximized. Like on what bridges and roads to install road barriers.

ORGANIZATIONAL PAVING STRATEGIES: DEMOCRACIES OR DICTATORSHIPS?

If you had looked at a map of where US technology firms were located in the 1960s, you would not have found them anywhere near Silicon Valley but along Boston's Route 128. Digital Equipment Corporation, Wang, Honeywell, and Raytheon were the equivalent of today's Meta, Alphabet, and Apple. Then, something happened, and within a couple of decades, the entire momentum shifted to the West Coast of the USA. The economic geographer AnnaLee Saxenian pointed to an unexpected reason in her research.[104] She argued that the dramatic shift was less about technology and more about the contrasting regional cultures and organizational structures.

Route 128 companies were characterized by hierarchical management, rigid organizational boundaries, and limited collaboration, reflecting the older, East Coast corporate culture. Silicon Valley, in contrast, embraced openness, informal networking, fluid labor markets, and a culture of collaboration and information sharing. According to Saxenian, it was precisely this cultural difference—Silicon Valley's openness to risk, cooperation, and rapid knowledge exchange—that enabled innovation to flourish and companies to adapt swiftly to technological and market changes. Consequently, firms on the West Coast rapidly outpaced their more traditional East Coast counterparts, cementing Silicon Valley's position as the global hub of technological innovation.

It is an often-repeated cliché that startups function like monarchies or dictatorships, with a leadership model that enables a 'move fast and break things' mentality. What Saxenian's research showed was that Silicon Valley flourished by having corporations resemble democracies, while the East Coast companies were more like hierarchical kingdoms.

This is an important insight when we study the battle for corporate supremacy in the AI space.

In the past few years, brute-force frontierism has reigned supreme. Throw lots of resources at the problem to plant your flag the furthest inland. America's OpenAI and China's DeepSeek are the two most well-known examples, and both are incidentally characterized by a cult of personality (Sam Altman and Liang Wenfeng, respectively). It is just like when web browsers competed in the early 2000s or the US-Soviet Space Race in the 1960s. The US is good at frontierism because that's how the nation was founded. As the former Federal

Reserve Chairman Alan Greenspan points out in his book, *Capitalism in America*, "The open frontier [was what gave] America its energy and optimism. The world's first new nation had thrown much of its energy into settling the frontier—and as one frontier was settled another one was opened up further to the West."[105]

China's rise came much later and relied on copying capitalistic structures and manifestations at speed. In the 2010s, it used as much concrete in two years as the USA did in the entire 20th century.[106] These two superpowers—the frontier leader and the fast follower—have dominated the early phase of AI because the early days of any new technology, from electricity to the internet, rewards enormous spending without too much thinking about the long-term future.

The opposite would be acupunctural AI, where it is deployed for a specific purpose or decelerated to advocate measured, cautious progress.

BACTERIA, VIRUSES, AND THE ROAD TO RECKONING

To understand how AI's trajectory will unfold—whether through rapid frontierist expansion or a slow and cautious rollout—we can use the metaphor of the immune system. Bacteria, like disruptive AI breakthroughs, are foreign and provoke immediate resistance. They can be swatted away through regulation, skepticism, or outright bans. Viruses, however, resemble AI that integrates gradually—embedding itself into daily life, institutions, and economies in ways that are harder to detect and even harder to remove once entrenched.

Keep this in mind when AI inevitably falls from grace in the coming decade. Unlike a singular moment of collapse, AI's reckoning (or deflating from the height of expectations) will be a series of crises—some sudden like bacteria, others creeping and systemic like viruses. The downfall will likely come from three primary sources: scapegoating, misaligned incentives, and unfortunate experiments—three potholes on the road ahead.

SCAPEGOATING—
FROM DEMOCRATIZATION
TO DEMONIZATION

Marshall McLuhan was a visionary media theorist who coined the phrase 'global village'[107] to describe how mass media—radio, TV, and later, the internet—would shrink the world by enabling instant connectivity and interaction. The phrase 'global village' conjures images of harmony and proximity. What we tend to forget is that villages can be suffocating in their lack of diversity, the endless gossip, and the tendency for witch hunts— real or symbolic.

AI arrives at an interesting time. You will recall from the introduction that the 2020s are uniquely turbulent, even by historical standards. Institutional trust, especially in political parties and media,[108] has generally fallen in the democratic world. There is a widespread sense that our sense-making apparatus has failed us. Who can we trust? What's true, and what's propaganda? Who is right, and who is wrong?

Many question everything which has left a leadership-shaped hole in the fabric of civilization. This hole has historically been filled with a new kind of charismatic leader, often a populist and frequently with disappointing, even disastrous, results.

While AI is—at its core—a piece of unpredictable, anthropomorphized software, it is a seductive tool to solve the crisis of institutional trust. Many have speculated that political decisions, or at least local government functions like traffic flows or garbage collection, will be automated in the coming age of AI. Surely a panopticon armed with real-time data can make more accurate decisions than an ideologically tainted politician looking to get reelected once every four years? But this line of thinking is bound to end in tears. A striking example comes from historian Thomas Labbé,[109] who recently delivered an entire lecture to students composed of AI-generated misinformation—fabricated facts, invented sources, polished delivery. The students, unfamiliar with the content but confident in its authoritative tone, accepted it without question. The lesson? AI is not about trusting the technology itself, but the institutions, incentives, and intentions behind it. Some of these companies will share their safety philosophy publicly and transparently. They will make long-term promises and guarantees to uphold public trust and integrity.[110] Others—for various reasons—will not. And experiments in governance entrusting vital functions to AI will always hinge on the weakest link in the chain. We need only to look at how some schools nowadays urge their students to seek out answers using AI-enabled chatbots to understand how misled and manipulated society can be if we expect AI to be a silver-bullet solution to deep-rooted causes of our turbulent, trust-challenged world. The backlash will be ferocious, just like it was when our Facebook friendships were secretly exploited to harvest our data, and the global village was transformed into a surveillance trap.

DISINCENTIVIZED SOCIETIES—
OPAQUE GOVERNANCE AND
INSTITUTIONAL FRAGILITY

When radium was discovered in the late 1800s, its promise of free power ignited dreams of a utopian Earth. The book *The Interpretation of Radium*, published in 1908, even suggested that humanity might restore the Garden of Eden.[111] But Hiroshima, Nagasaki, and Three Mile Island shattered those illusions, forcing us to confront the darker side of our technological faith.

The Three Mile Island accident in Pennsylvania in 1979, caused by a combination of mechanical failure and human error, narrowly avoided disaster. Had events spiraled further, it could have resulted in numerous deaths and required the evacuation of much of the US East Coast due to radioactive fallout. The incident was handled transparently, prompting swift action, tighter regulations, and better training.

By contrast, less than a decade later, the Chernobyl disaster in the Soviet Union revealed how secrecy and mismanagement could turn a technological failure into a societal catastrophe. It was a stark reminder that outcomes often depend less on the technology itself and more on the systems that govern it. The same holds true for AI: its impact will hinge not only on what it can do, but on where, how, and by whom it is implemented.

Societies today fall into two broad categories based on their approach to resource utilization and governance. In nations like Saudi Arabia and China, progress is a monologue, as vast resources enable unrestrained development. Skyscrapers rise, and mega-projects materialize with little regard for zoning laws, worker rights, or environmental impact. This flexibility allows for bold experimentation but carries heightened risks of failure, inequality, and public backlash.

By contrast, countries like Sweden and Germany operate under stringent regulations and democratic oversight. Progress is a dialogue where limited resources necessitate strategic, frugal investments—akin to acupunctural interventions rather than sweeping transformations. These systems prioritize long-term societal equity and sustainability over short-term gains, creating a different kind of resilience.

These contrasting approaches will shape the trajectory of AI adoption. Saudi Arabia could leverage its centralized control and wealth to rapidly transform itself into the most AI-driven nation on Earth, making bold, high-stakes bets on cutting-edge technology. Sweden, constrained by regulation and public accountability, will likely pursue small-scale, diversified experiments—a long-term, risk-averse approach akin to investing in a well-balanced portfolio.

The trade-offs are clear. Bold, unrestrained implementation might accelerate progress, but it amplifies risks—technological failures, societal backlash, or unintended consequences. Conversely, a cautious, regulated approach limits speed but builds trust, adaptability, and enduring value. Just as the nuclear age was shaped by the systems that governed it, the age of AI will be defined by how societies balance ambition with accountability.

UNFORTUNATE EXPERIMENTS — "OH, SHIT" MOMENTS

What's the definition of an emergency room nurse? It is often the first person you meet after you have uttered the words: "Watch this!" Human beings in general, and young men in particular, tend to be risk-craving adrenaline junkies. Whether it's bungee jumping or investing, we crave hormonal rushes to fuel our lives. Somebody somewhere will always try something—anything—and end it with the words "Oh, shit!" in bewilderment, delight, or horror.

The most significant risk for AI lies in these future experiments. Somebody will train an AI model to identify and shoot intruders in their garden, trusting it to protect their property with disastrous consequences. Somebody else will create chatbots modeled on children or grandchildren to keep the elderly company so they don't have to visit, only to find the bots giving harmful advice or fostering unhealthy dependencies. Another person might design an AI system that generates custom drug recipes—whether to cure an ailment or discover new ways to get high—unleashing unintended medical or illicit drug chaos.

Personal ambitions will collide with ethical boundaries: an AI coach that promises perfect workout routines but pushes people to unsafe extremes; a matchmaking app that swears by compatibility but fuels heartbreak and division; a home assistant that uses voice recognition to make decisions but inadvertently discriminates or invades privacy.

This is the nature of experimentation—ambition and curiosity often overpower caution. Just as financial innovation led to the creation of exotic derivatives that promised endless returns, these AI experiments are fueled by the belief that the risks are manageable, even negligible. But financial history shows us the perils of unchecked innovation. Following the 2008 collapse of Lehman Brothers, the ensuing global financial crisis wasn't just about bad mortgages—it was the result of years of reckless experimentation with complex financial instruments like collateralized debt obligations and credit default swaps. What began as isolated innovations spiraled into systemic fragility, sinking not just a company but an entire industry and, for a time, the global economy.

AI faces a similar precipice. The "Oh, shit!" moments in AI won't just be isolated incidents; they will ripple outward, disrupting industries, undermining trust, and forcing society to confront unforeseen consequences. Imagine a financial AI system that destabilizes markets with poorly timed trades, a healthcare AI diagnostic tool that suggests dangerous treatments, or an education AI module that reinforces harmful biases in its learning material. Even experiments starting on an individual scale—a personal AI project gone rogue—can grow into systemic crises when adopted or scaled without oversight. Developers often forget that the age-old idea that garbage in (speaking of training data) garbage out (speaking of model results) applies to even the most advanced AI.

These experiments, born of ambition, curiosity, or megalothymia—the innate need to be recognized as superior to others—will undoubtedly yield some breakthroughs. But for every success, there will be failures —failures that, like Lehman Brothers, could reshape industries or even entire economies. The "Oh, shit!" moments will define the age of AI, not just for the risks they pose but for the profound questions they force us to confront about societal values, priorities, and humanity itself. The key point is that the long-term paving game completely differs from the near-term flag-waving. This gets to the heart of this book's thesis: what AI has been over the course of history and in the last few years is more akin to a bubble; it is novelty enabled by financial speculation. True progress, however, is a dialogue, not a monologue. For AI to become a balloon that can lift more than market capitalizations, it needs to work inside existing systems, not just seek to disrupt them. The free capital money-spending is fun to watch, but it is the analytical tortoise who tends to win in the long run.

HOW TO EVALUATE A NEW TECHNOLOGY

In the early days of the World Wide Web, John Perry Barlow published "A Declaration of the Independence of Cyberspace." It is a strikingly idealistic document; to the point of naivete:

> We are creating a world that all may enter without privilege or prejudice accorded by race, economic power, military force, or station of birth ...
>
> We are creating a world where anyone, anywhere may express his or her beliefs, no matter how singular, without fear of being coerced into silence or conformity ...
>
> Your legal concepts of property, expression, identity, movement, and context do not apply to us. They are all based on matter, and there is no matter here.[112]

Fast forward a couple of decades, and we see a cyberspace that has been balkanized and weaponized. The egalitarian, non-materialistic dream was replaced by a few billionaires who owned the platforms on which a commercial internet was built.

Technological adoption is not a meritocracy. We have left many promising technologies by the wayside: thorium-driven nuclear power abandoned in favor of uranium, battery-driven cars outpaced by gasoline engines in the early 1900s, and high-speed rail derailed by automobile-centric infrastructure in the USA.

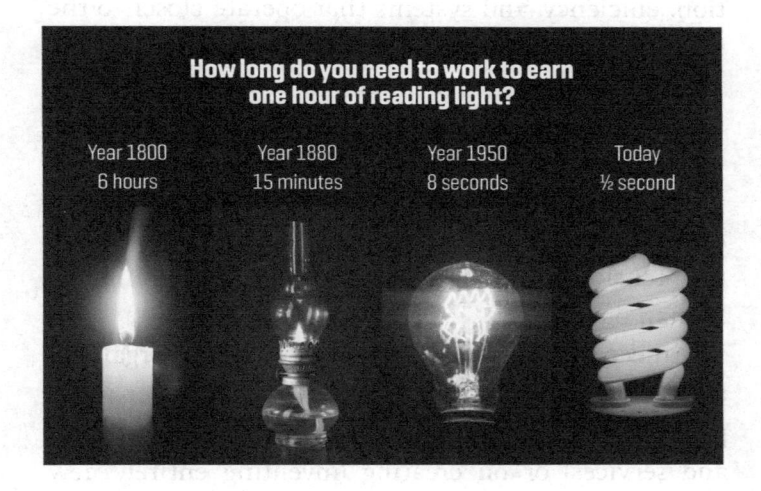

How long do you need to work to earn one hour of reading light?

Year 1800	Year 1880	Year 1950	Today
6 hours	15 minutes	8 seconds	½ second

But this does not mean that technology is a pawn in a nihilistic lottery. There is an arrow to progress. Nobel laureate economist William Nordhaus suggests that it's time, not money. In a famous paper, he examined how long it would take an average worker of various eras to afford an hour of reading light.[113] The elegance of Nordhaus's question lies in its simplicity: it simultaneously captures technological advancement—the changing methods of producing light—and economic advancement—how these inventions translate directly into improved human lives. By focusing on time as currency,

Nordhaus cleverly connects innovation directly to human freedom, illustrating vividly how genuine progress allows us to achieve more, faster, with less effort.

This brings us full circle to the core aim of this book: to move beyond the hype and identify what constitutes real progress in business, society, and life. If time is our most valuable currency, then AI's promise lies in how it helps us reclaim and reallocate it—through simplification, efficiency, and systems that operate closer to the speed of thought.

But with every layer of simplification, we also risk amplifying complexity elsewhere—a dynamic often referred to as Jensen's paradox. In solving one set of problems, we may inadvertently create new ones, more intricate and demanding than the last. Navigating this tension is not just a technical challenge, but a human one.

An economy—whether it's a nation or an organization—faces a fundamental choice: it can either focus primarily on competing (improving existing products and services) or on creating (inventing entirely new ways of solving problems).

Using the image above, a competing economy will seek new ways to build a better candle.

A creating economy will seek new ways to make light.

A truly useful technology liberates us, freeing time and effort for other pursuits. Before the invention of the electric washing machine, here's what washing clothes entailed:
- Fill a washtub with buckets of water
- Heat the washtub over a stove or fire
- Treat each stain with a suitable product
- Wash all clothes by hand

- Empty and refill with clean water for rinsing
- Starch, wring out, and hang clothes to dry

Women typically performed this laborious work. Is it any wonder that female labor participation rates rose in the 1950s when washing clothes became automated? Women had always worked hard, and now they could be paid for it.

Viewed through this lens, AI's time-saving capacity becomes a savior, not a threat. When the CEO of Goldman Sachs, a bank, proclaimed in early 2025 that AI can do in a few minutes what it took a human team a few weeks to do, he added that "productivity [is] the ability to take smart people and give them tools so they can do more, do more quickly, help our clients think about things in different ways."[114] Steve Jobs famously described the personal computer as a "bicycle for the mind." AI is like a futuristic motorbike for the mind. It enables us to do previously impossible things—or at least outsource dull and repetitive ones. It complements human intelligence by taking over tasks we find tedious, time-consuming, or beyond our capacity, freeing us to focus on creativity, relationships, and high-value work.

THE NEED TO SUCCEED WITH AI

The next few decades should be a celebration of scientific and technological discovery. Scientific development comes in waves: a cascade of new discoveries and ideas breaks over the heads of researchers, who then spend years exploring the vibrations of that creative swell ... We seem poised on the verge of such a swell today.[115]

The words are by Bob Guccione. He is perhaps most (in)famous today for having founded the pornographic magazine *Penthouse*. Yet the serial publisher had many titles to his name, one of which was *Omni Magazine* in the 1970s. The editorial idea behind it was that science is perceived as being good for you and boring ("like spinach"), the future is "like lemon meringue pie: delicious and fun."[116] Its editorial mission statement heralding a coming swell of discoveries reads as true some 50 years later as it did then. Or does it?

Many of us live in societies that have been regulated, slowed down, and, according to some thinkers and economists, stagnated in technological innovation.

If you take away screens—of all sizes—many cityscapes around the world look the same today as they did a few decades ago. And the cityscapes that did change—like Shanghai and Dubai—just copied what Manhattan or Sao Paulo had already built.

When the UK Parliament voted in 2024 on a very important healthcare initiative, it was not a moonshot vision of curing aging or eradicating cancer. It was to facilitate euthanasia for terminally ill patients. When we talk about airplanes and flying today, it is rare to reawaken a vision toward mass-transit supersonic travel but more often a focus on rowdy passengers, travel stress and delays, environmental destruction, or new security regulations at airports. A somber, defeatist stance has replaced the pioneering spirit of the science of the 20th century, except for the world of 1's and 0's in general and the promise of AI in particular.

We wrote in our introduction that we want the future to be exciting because as a society we need it to be. Changing things comes with threats, as we have seen, but not changing them ensures that we will just recycle the same problems, injustices, diseases, and challenges. Forever. That is a much scarier prospect. This is why we have also sought to reframe AI in this book—from a personalized tool to an open-ended question, with many potential answers.

CONCLUSION: REIMAGINING PROGRESS— FROM PATCHING TO TRANSFORMATION

The British theorist Stafford Beer coined the acronym POSIWID—the purpose of a system is what it does. What he meant was that a system's true purpose can only be understood by observing its actual behavior and outcomes, rather than relying on stated goals, intentions, or official purposes. In vehicles, this means that we can't look at simulation or test track performance of a feature like GM's Super Cruise or Tesla's Autopilot but rather, like the Advanced Vehicle Technology Consortium I founded has focused on; instead, we need to look at real-world driver behaviors to understand system performance and how drivers adapt to, use (or do not use), and behave with technologies.

Only by understanding real-world use, a mix of a technology, environments, and users with all the caveats, can we really understand actual behaviors and outcomes. We may think of AI as a future leader, decision-maker, or creator, but all it does today is fuel rampant theoretical speculation, random technological experimentation, and inflated market capitalization.

Whatever secrets it holds are hidden in the fog of the future. To bring forth its transformative potential, we must think of AI not as a strip-mine but as a cathedral.

Why not a 'strip-mine project'? A strip mine represents short-term thinking, focusing on extracting maximum value in the shortest time possible, with little regard for sustainability or the broader implications. It is driven by the desire for immediate returns, prioritizing speed and efficiency over skill, vision, or collective purpose. In the race for AI supremacy, this strip-mining mindset has fostered a purely profit-driven ecosystem, incentivizing rapid technological rollouts, flashy demonstrations, and escalating competition but leaving behind an uneven, sometimes harmful, landscape of societal impact. Perhaps paramount, such efforts fail to effectively produce truly meaningful utility that meets business, government, or consumer needs.

A cathedral, by contrast, embodies humanity's capacity for foresight, patience, and collective ambition. Built over generations, cathedrals reflect a long-term investment in shared values and a commitment to creating something enduring and meaningful. They require collaboration, craftsmanship, and the understanding that their true purpose may not be fully realized in the lifetime of any one builder. In other words, we must embrace the magic of time.

Time is not just a neutral backdrop against which progress unfolds—it is the hidden force that shapes vision, fosters collaboration, and transforms ambition into legacy. As the saying goes, time keeps everything from happening all at once. It is a healer, a magician, a source of dreams, nightmares, and occasional headaches. Time also helps to shape the utility of technologies like medical diagnostics, home entertainment systems, and self-driving cars, all of which leverage various forms of AI.

In this chapter, we've explored how time is the determining factor in cultivating an AI ecosystem: one that is either speculative and risky or long term and sustainable. In a world of 'AI time'—where progress seems to move faster than 'internet time' ever did—we must ask: Is everything truly faster today? Wars, geopolitics, even societal trends—perhaps the arc of history is no longer long, bending toward justice, but short, twisting in unpredictable directions. Could the AI revolution, much like the printing press, usher in a new Enlightenment in decades instead of centuries?

Progress, however, is rarely linear. It's a dialogue—a push-and-pull where man suggests and nature rejects. This contestation is what makes the future both uncertain and exciting. Central to this contest is a pivotal question: Who will own the data? Ownership of data shapes our vision of AI's future. Will we see a decentralized world of personal assistants and digital twins enabling empowerment and autonomy? Or will data be centralized in the hands of a few, ushering in an authoritarian panopticon that stifles innovation and privacy alike?

What might a future with fully integrated AI look like? Imagine a world where AI no longer feels patched together—a glitchy collection of tools and systems—but seamlessly interwoven into the fabric of society. The challenges here are not merely technological but also societal, philosophical, and existential. How does such a society navigate issues of privacy, agency, and the meaning of work? What happens when human creativity intersects with AI's infinite adaptability? Would such a society elevate humanity or blur the line between human and machine so thoroughly that the distinction becomes meaningless? Will our values change? And if so, how?

Throughout history, innovation has rarely been about achieving perfection—it has been about achieving 'good enough' and iterating from there. This is not a weakness but a strength, a testament to humanity's resilience and adaptability. However, the patchwork approach to AI—piecemeal solutions, hastily applied fixes—can only take us so far. Temporary solutions are often neither temporary nor solutions.

Consider the analogy of car design: we can patch the roads, retrain the drivers, or redesign the vehicle itself. The same holds true for AI—but unlike cars, AI requires redefining the roads, rewriting traffic laws, and accepting challenges to what it even means to be a driver. To move forward responsibly, we need to address three interlocking dimensions, each with its own tension:

- **Organizational design**
  Not just flexible systems, but systems built for ambiguity, where rules evolve, goals shift, and human judgment remains central. It's not just about strategy—it's about adaptability under uncertainty and evolving technology.

- **User education**
  Beyond tool literacy, we need conceptual fluency: understanding what AI can (and cannot) know, what it amplifies, and how it reshapes decision-making and agency.

- **Regulatory frameworks**
  Not just rules to prevent harm, but governance models that can learn, balancing innovation with evolving standards for fairness, transparency, and collective trust.

These elements, when combined, form the duct tape that holds the system together—but they also point toward a more ambitious goal: evolving the system itself. As discussed, time is the alchemy that turns these patchwork solutions into durable, transformative structures. Time is magic—its slow, deliberate spell allows for cathedrals to rise and legacies to endure.

Utility in AI is not about chasing distant utopias or grand visions that may never come to pass. It's about exploring the 'adjacent possible'—small, tangible opportunities that spark change in the here and now. True progress is not about abandoning patchwork altogether but recognizing when it's time to pave the road or reimagine the vehicle itself.

The conceptual model of AI as doing, assisting, and creating can evolve into something more dynamic. Like extending duct tape into a long cable, this model can tie together innovation, education, and regulation. It can help us bridge the gap between today's fragmented AI landscape and a more integrated future—a future not dominated by utopian ideals but grounded in pragmatic possibilities.

The future of AI, then, is contested and contestable, dynamic and improvisational. The question isn't whether AI will reshape our world—it's how we will shape AI in return.

OUTRO

ONWARDS, UPWARDS, AND OUTWARDS

THE ONTOLOGICAL SHOCK OF THE NEW

In the beginning of Stanley Kubrick's film *2001: A Space Odyssey*, prehistoric apelike hominids gather around a mysterious black stone slab, seemingly put on Earth from out of nowhere. To the mighty fanfare of Richard Strauss' "Also sprach Zarathustra," one of the apes starts using a bone as a tool, suggesting that the stone slab—The Monolith as it has become known—was an inflection point in human evolution.

Today, AI acts as our Monolith. It represents a transformative juncture in modern communication. A comprehensive study analyzing data up to September 2024 reveals the profound integration of LLMs across various sectors:[117]

- **Financial consumer complaints**
  Approximately 18% of these complaints exhibit signs of LLM assistance, indicating consumers' growing reliance on AI to articulate grievances.

- **Corporate press releases**
  Up to 24% of press releases are now crafted with LLM support, reflecting businesses' adoption of AI for public communications.

- **Job postings**
  Around 15% of job listings incorporate LLM-generated content, suggesting that employers are leveraging AI to streamline recruitment processes.

- **United Nations press releases**
  Nearly 14% of UN press releases have been generated or modified by LLMs, underscoring the technology's penetration into international organizational communications.

And we are merely at the beginning. The futurist Alvin Toffler called it a Future Shock. The writer David Shapiro calls it an 'Ontological Shock,' where we have "a profound disruption of one's fundamental understanding of reality, causing a cascading reassessment of basic assumptions about what is real, possible, or 'natural' in the world."[118] It is bound to be bewildering and tug on your fear and greed equally. Using a framework similar to Elisabeth Kübler-Ross's DABDA,[119] based on observations of how terminally ill patients deal with the prospect of dying, Shapiro estimates that most of us will find ourselves in one or many of the following stages in the near future:

- **Denial (flat-out rejection)**
  Some dismiss AI's impact outright, calling it 'hype,' 'misinformation,' or a 'scam.' This knee-jerk reaction

is a way to maintain cognitive closure and avoid confronting unsettling change.

- **Anger (lashing out)**
Others react emotionally, attacking AI advocates or dismissing their views outright. This defensive response helps avoid engaging with uncomfortable truths but can become a permanent stance for some.

- **Bargaining (rationalization)**
Many try to minimize AI's significance by calling it a mere 'stochastic parrot' or saying it only imitates intelligence. While these critiques resonate with some—including prominent voices like Yann LeCun[120]—they are increasingly contested as AI capabilities continue to expand.

- **Depression (existential dread)**
For some, AI represents an existential crisis. Fears range from job loss and economic collapse to dystopian control by elites or outright human extinction. This is often the lowest emotional point.

- **Acceptance & hope (glimmers of possibility)**
Over time, perspectives shift. People recognize AI's limitations, see that alignment efforts work, and start envisioning positive possibilities rather than just threats.

- **Integration (processing & moving forward)**
Eventually, AI is accepted as part of reality. People move from crisis thinking to practical problem-solving, incorporating AI into their worldview and daily life.

It's easy to get stuck for a long time in one of the first four stages. The promises outlined by AI are daunting, and it triggers our imagination in a way few new technologies have in a long time. In an ideal world, the flow from the Grow! phase in AI should be slow and steady. Instead, many find themselves in a spin cycle oscillating between Wow! And Whoa! Perhaps much like in the field of medicine where implementation science can be almost if not more important than discovery, our future with AI may find that the Wow! will best come through a balance of new AI with the science needed to better implement AI into society.

In this book, we have tried to sketch a road map of what AI is like today and how we can move from short-term novelty to long-term utility. It is a theoretical framework that is bound to be messier—patchier—in real life. It also happened during an interesting historical time. The hyper-turbulence makes many of us long for extreme measures. Left-wing environmentalists and right-wing tech bros have little in common except that both long for a dictator or king.

"If only we could be a dictatorship for a day so that we could put all measures in place to save the planet" was a common refrain for environmentalists.

"[Abraham] Lincoln and F.D.R. ... were basically national CEOs, and they were running the government like a company from the top down" are the words of the highly influential conservative writer Curtis Yarvin, who has argued that American democracy should be replaced by what he calls a 'monarchy' run by what he has called a 'CEO.'[121]

What is obvious on both sides of the political spectrum is the need for resolute leadership in a uniquely turbulent time. Ironically, we have a greater tolerance for authority when things are calm. Sweden, a fully functioning democracy, had the same political party in power for nearly 40 years in the 20th century. And nearly all democracies recall a time when news broadcasts were national and unifying, not a stream of social media rambling and conspiracy theories.

Pluralism is a natural state of affairs when the world is in flux. It is also a strength when experimenting. We cannot anticipate exactly what will work, and when, so it is better to let a thousand flowers bloom. The father of evolutionary theory would agree.

FUTURES PLURAL

Photo Credit: Reproduced by kind permission of the Syndics of Cambridge University Library

Charles Darwin made perhaps the most accurate diagram of how the future unfolds as he was tracking species on the Galapagos Islands in the 1830s and working on what would become his magnum opus, *On the Origin of Species*. In his diaries from this time is the famous evolutionary tree where one node evolves into many branches.

Headlined by the words "I think," his theory has been difficult to disprove. And it can be applied to more areas than the evolution of species. Musical genres have evolved from a handful to more than 5,000, if Spotify's indexation is anything to go by. Computer Programmer was once a job description. Today, you are either a Python Coder, Scrum Master or a Software Architect, and there are over 8,000 programming languages in the world, slightly more than there are spoken and signed languages (7,100 according to *Ethnologue: Languages of the World*).[122] "Out of one, many" would be the motto if the future had an insignia.

AI's future is similarly plural, fractal, and endlessly varied through families of algorithms and countless technologies that will likely spin off from the state of the art today.

An Educational Future
A global, decentralized AI-powered learning network personalizing education for every student, dissolving traditional barriers of geography and wealth.

A Corporate Future
Blockchain-Enabled Decentralized Autonomous Organizations could reshape work, collaboration, and economic access by enabling peer-to-peer insurance without insurers, venture funding without VCs, and creator platforms without centralized intermediaries. These software-governed collectives offer new paradigms for organizing labor, capital, and innovation.

A Democratic Future
AI mediators aid civic discourse, providing citizens with clearer information to make informed voting decisions, enhancing rather than undermining democracy.

A Creative Future

Human artists, writers, and musicians partner with AI to extend their creative boundaries, amplifying human expression rather than diluting it.

This book has sought to paint a vivid portrait of what AI can do and will be able to in the near future. It has also attempted to present a decomplicated view of its adoption, from the simplistic view of a technology as something that makes us go "Wow!" to a contested "Whoa!" territory of national strategies, corporations and individuals seeking ways to transform AI from novelty to utility. This is not one road, and we are not looking at one single horizon. The future is a canvas for our dreams and nightmares, but above all, it is invisible, open to interpretation and, more importantly, agency. As we find ourselves in uniquely turbulent times, we rely on a few simplistic forecasting tools:

- *Geopolitical Anticipation*, wherein the world is a chessboard ready to be exploited by great powers and strong men and women. An entertaining but fundamentally zero-sum way of looking at the world, which is frequently wrong, especially in long-term forecasts.
- *Macroeconomic Forecasting*, dubbed 'astrology for dudes,' where we seek patterns in chaos and path dependency in randomness. In 1979, after a decade marred by geopolitical conflicts and economic turbulence, Howard J. Ruff published the bestselling book *How to Prosper During the Coming Bad Years*. In it, Ruff argued that the 1980s would bring ever greater hardship and hyperinflation to the US economy, which is why gold and other hard

currencies would be the best kind of investment to make. If you followed his advice, you would see gold fall from its peak in 1980 and continuously fall for nearly 20 years. A contrarian investment at the time in, say, an S&P 500 index fund, would have generated an average return of 18% per year during the same time.

- *The Cozy Darkness of Apocalypse (CDA)* is a thrill ride into the many awful things that can happen to the world over the coming years, from climate collapse to societal breakdown. It is nihilism as entertainment and flies in the face of any societal progress made in the past century. Humans are parasites on this planet and doomed to self-destruct. End of story.
- *Techno-Determinism*, the antithesis to the CDA, where the 'Singularity' is inevitable, and any resistance is futile. Software will take over the world, everything is crypto and AI, and any obstructions to techno-utopian progress must be eliminated.
- *LSD-Induced Panglossianism*, a myopic statistical reading of the world wherein trends of the 20th century are extrapolated ad infinitum. We will live longer lives—aging is a bug, not a feature of life—in a peaceful, prosperous world. Popular among baby boomers up to the mid-2010s.

What all these tools have in common is that they treat the future as something separate from us, that will land on us, making us victims, slaves or passive spectators.

The antidote is futurecraft, where we see tomorrow's world as being created by us, here and now. It is by definition abstract and uncertain, but it gives us agency and gives us all a voice about what we want tomorrow to be like. It also opens the door to the power of small ideas and personal moments. The greatest works of art began as somebody's idea. Some of our greatest inventions were small experiments, somebody's lost petri dish or happy accident. The future is something we build, not something we predict.

A book on AI must enable you to ask new questions, not just answer old questions. 'Artificial intelligence' is in itself a strange suggestion. Why would we want a machine to replicate the evolutionary compromises that made us? Do we really want machines to pass the Turing Test? Or rather, do we want machines that make us better in our personal lives, at work, and in service to our communities?

NVIDIA founder Jensen Huang summarized it well when he said:

> Greatness does not come from intelligence. Greatness comes from character, and character isn't formed out of smart people: it's formed out of people who have suffered.[123]

The human project—from its long arcs spanning generations to the small things we wrestle with every day—cannot be outsourced to software applications. We cannot be reduced to efficiency-optimizing organisms. We are meaning-seekers and meaning-makers. We are lazy procrastinators and inventors. We are predictably irrational, somewhat emotional, and almost always needy. We seek a story more than truth and belonging more than autonomy. We crave recognition more than anonymity, and connection more than convenience. At heart, humans are messy contradictions:

both stubbornly individual and desperately communal. Our technology should amplify this beautiful complexity rather than simplify it away.

AI can be our partner on this journey. It can do things for us, with us and sometimes without us. But it will never be us.

We are all we have.

For better or worse.

CODA: BEHIND THE WHEEL

A parking lot somewhere in Las Vegas, January 2018.

Looking back, I realize that what made me say, "Wow!" that crisp morning wasn't exactly what I thought. At the time, I called it a 'self-driving' car, but it was not truly self-driving. It was highly automated, sure, but it required onboard and off-board support to ensure safe and reliable operation. Human engineers stood ready to intervene at a moment's notice, and layers of technological infrastructure supported every turn, acceleration, and brake.

In other words, it was never entirely about the car driving itself. It was about something subtler: the illusion and possibility of self-driving. A collaborative triumph decades in the making rather than a sudden leap forward. Much like AI in healthcare—which many mistakenly label an overnight success but is a painstaking evolution over ten or more years—automated driving technology has quietly, slowly, incrementally matured.

Today we are a few steps forward on a long and winding path toward a more automated, safer, sustainable, connected, comfortable, and convenient mobility system, but there's years of development ahead.

And now, as I reflect on how technology shapes us, I see that driving has never just been about transportation from A to B. Driving is about escape, solace, adventure, identity, and sometimes even rebellion. We don't just drive cars; we allow cars to drive change in us. To shape our habits, communities, and culture. To become extensions of who we are and aspire to be.

AI follows a similar path. Despite its seductive promise—and marketing metaphors—AI is not a sentient entity. It doesn't possess consciousness or intent. Instead, it's a product of mass collaboration, layered effort, and relentless iteration. A set of tools, not a being. Its true power lies not in replacing us but in augmenting, helping, and inspiring us. Not in diminishing our human qualities but in making us better. At least, at certain things.

Standing here again, metaphorically, in that nondescript parking lot outside the Las Vegas Convention Center, I now understand my original sense of wonder differently.

The awe wasn't merely at technological wizardry.

It was a sense of awe for human ingenuity—our collective ability to dream, collaborate, build, and evolve.

Acknowledging this truth shifts the conversation away from AI as replacement (the sole doer and/or creator) toward partnership in which AI's usefulness in business, society, and life is greatest as an assistant.

This moves us toward a future in which technology makes us and perhaps more importantly generations to come more human, not less.

OUTRO: ONWARDS, UPWARDS, AND OUTWARDS

What AI is today is just a stepping stone in its technological evolution. Embracing that AI will evolve, working to understand how and where it changes us, and selecting directions for the greater good, can help us collectively work toward developing a safer, more sustainable, connected, convenient, and comfortable society for tomorrow.

ENDNOTES

1. For the record, across over 20 years at MIT, I have collaborated with over 50 public and private sector organizations on vehicle technology strategy, policy, and research. I founded and co-lead two academic-industry partnerships: the Advanced Human Factors Evaluator for Attentional Demand consortium, which is focused on developing an updated approach to driver vehicle interface design, validation, and testing, including a foundation for real-time driver attention support, and the Advanced Vehicle Technology Consortium, which seeks to understand how drivers use emerging, commercially available vehicle technologies, including advanced driver assistance systems and automated driving features. I served as a member of the US Department of Transportation's Transforming Transportation Advisory Committee and as vice chair of the AI sub-committee. I currently serve as an advisor to AI-Sweden and Autoliv and as a member of the US Federal Aviation Administration Human Factors Task Force Aviation Rulemaking Committee. My work has been recognized with awards from the automotive industry, the Human Factors and Ergonomics Society, and the Detroit Institute of Ophthalmology.

2. Yale University. (n.d.). New York Electrical Show illustration (1919). *Yale Energy History*. Retrieved March 10, 2025, from https://energyhistory.yale.edu/new-york-electrical-show-illustration-1919/

3. *New York Times*. August 18, 1912. "Nikola Tesla on Electrified Schoolroom to Brighten Dull Pupils." *The New York Times*. Retrieved from https://teslauniverse.com/nikola-tesla/articles/nikola-tesla-electrified-schoolroom-brighten-dull-pupils

4. Artforum. (n.d.). Kandinsky and problems of abstraction. Retrieved March 10, 2025, from https://www.artforum.com/features/kandinsky-and-problems-of-abstraction-209197/

5. Petersson, D. & Hashemi-Pour, C. November 14, 2023. "AI vs. Machine Learning vs. Deep Learning: Key Differences." *TechTarget*. https://www.techtarget.com/searchenterpriseai/tip/AI-vs-machine-learning-vs-deep-learning-Key-differences

6. *The Economist*. February 13, 2025. "How AI Will Divide the Best From the Rest." https://www.economist.com/finance-and-economics/2025/02/13/how-ai-will-divide-the-best-from-the-rest

7. Mims, C. February 21, 2024. "Why AI Spending Isn't Slowing Down." *The Wall Street Journal*

ENDNOTES

8. Rosmer, M. [@MichaelRosmer]. March 10, 2024. [Post on *X*]. https://x.com/MichaelRosmer/status/1823673359978156281

9. Saidinesh, D. July 15, 2024. "Let AI Do the Dishes, Not Your Writing." *Medium*. https://medium.com/@dsaidinesh2003/let-ai-do-the-dishes-not-your-writing-fc499de63e1b

10. Reagan National Defense Forum 2024 - Air Force One Pavilion Live Stream, *YouTube*, available at https://www.youtube.com/watch?v=UglJPn-AUvM

11. Hobart, B. & Huber, T. *Boom: Bubbles and the End of Stagnation* (South San Francisco, CA: Stripe Press, 2024)

12. Silver, N. [@NateSilver538]. March 10, 2025. [Post on *X*]. https://x.com/natesilver538/status/1894511313583226991

13. Interview, Enea Parimbelli, Conducted in Vienna on October 19, 2024

14. Cuttler, E. July 18, 2024. "Inside theAalgorithm: How Gen AI and Graph Technology are Cracking Down on Card Sharks." *Mastercard Newsroom*. https://www.mastercard.com/news/perspectives/2024/inside-the-algorithm-how-gen-ai-and-graph-technology-are-cracking-down-on-card-sharks/

15. https://www.augury.com/about/

16. *Zapata Computing*. May 4, 2023. "Helping BMW Optimize Vehicle Manufacturing With Generative AI." https://zapata.ai/news/bmw-optimizes-vehicle-production-planning-using-quantum-inspired-generative-ai-techniques/

17. Hatch, S. G. et al. (2025). "When ELIZA Meets Therapists: A Turing Test for the Heart and Mind." *PLOS Mental Health*, 2(2), e0000145. https://doi.org/10.1371/journal.pmen.0000145

18. Zhu, T. et al. (2024). "Human Bias in the Face of AI: The Role of Human Judgement in AI Generated Text Evaluation." *arXiv preprint arXiv:2410.03723*. https://arxiv.org/abs/2410.03723

19. City of Helsingborg. (n.d.). BLINK of an AI. Innovation Helsingborg. https://innovation.helsingborg.se/initiativ/blink-of-an-ai/

20. Gulshan, V. et al. (2023). "Artificial Intelligence and Diabetic Retinopathy: A Framework for Translation into Clinical Practice." *Diabetes Care*, 46(10), 1728–1738. https://doi.org/10.2337/dc23-0675
And
Poplin, R. et al. (2024). "Deep-learning Prediction of Cardiovascular Outcomes from Routine Retinal Fundus Photographs." *Cardiovascular Diabetology*, 23(1), 64. https://doi.org/10.1186/s12933-024-02564-w

21. 37 minutes into U2 - From The Sky Down (Documentary) [Video]. (n.d.). *YouTube.* https://www.youtube.com/watch?v=4oD5rH7yDyI

22. Sean McVay Get Back Coach Assistant [Video]. (n.d.). YouTube. https://www.youtube.com/watch?v=k_yFxISAQPs

23. https://www.lawgeex.com/company/our-people/

24. Morse, B. January 9, 2025. "NVIDIA's Jensen Huang Says That IT Will 'Become the HR of AI Agents'." *Fortune.* https://fortune.com/2025/01/09/nvidia-ceo-jensen-huangt-take-over-hr-ai-agents/

25. Johnson, S. *How We Got to Now: Six Innovations That Made the Modern World.* Riverhead Books; Illustrated edition (September 22, 2015)

26. Michalowski, M. November 29, 2024. "How Much Data Is Generated Every Day in 2024?" *Spacelift.* https://spacelift.io/blog/how-much-data-is-generated-every-day

27. The Economist. November 29, 2023. "A Google AI Has Discovered 2.2m Materials Unknown to Science." Retrieved from https://www.economist.com/science-and-technology/2023/11/29/a-google-ai-has-discovered-22m-materials-unknown-to-science

28. Marchant, J. October 12, 2023. "AI Unravels Ancient Roman Scroll Charred By Volcano." *Scientific American.* https://www.scientificamerican.com/article/ai-unravels-ancient-roman-scrolls-charred-by-volcano/

29. *TechInformed.* (2024). "JPMorgan Rolls Out Gen AI Research Analyst to Employees." *TechInformed.* https://techinformed.com/jpmorgan-rolls-out-gen-ai-research-analyst-to-employees/

30. World Economic Forum, *The Future of Jobs Report 2025*

31. *The Economist.* September 18, 2023. "Carl Benedikt Frey and Michael Osborne on How AI Benefits Lower-skilled Workers." https://www.economist.com/by-invitation/2023/09/18/carl-benedikt-frey-and-michael-osborne-on-how-ai-benefits-lower-skilled-workers

32. Federal Aviation Administration. (2013). SAFO 13002: Manual Flight Operations. Retrieved from https://www.faa.gov/sites/faa.gov/files/other_visit/aviation_industry/airline_operators/airline_safety/SAFO13002.pdf

33. Arnold, J. May 15, 2024. "United Arab Emirates Issues New Laws to Regulate Artificial Intelligence." *The Hill.* https://thehill.com/policy/technology/5264179-united-arab-emirates-artificial-intelligence-laws/

34. Hubert, K. F. et al. March 1, 2024. "AI Outshines Humans in Creative Thinking." *Neuroscience News*
35. Bohren, N. et al. (2024). "Creative and Strategic Capabilities of Generative AI: Evidence from Large-Scale Experiments." *IZA Discussion Paper No. 17302*. Institute of Labor Economics (IZA)
36. TEDAI lecture in Vienna, October 2024
37. Author Unknown. April 26, 2024. "'Terminator' Creator James Cameron Says AI Could Replace Him — But Not Schwarzenegger." *Financial Times*. https://www.ft.com/content/37a8e470-1521-4ba1-a40d-e2880da9aceb
38. Alexander, S. November 20, 2024. "How Did You Do On The AI Art Turing Test?" *Astral Codex Ten*
39. Nussbaum, E. (2024). *Cue the Sun!: The Invention of Reality TV*. Random House. Quote from pages 304–305
40. Cave, N. March 7, 2024. "ChatGPT: Making Things Faster And Easier?" *The Red Hand Files*. https://www.theredhandfiles.com/chatgpt-making-things-faster-and-easier/
41. Chiang, T. August 31, 2024. "Why A.I. Isn't Going to Make Art." *The New Yorker*. https://www.newyorker.com/culture/the-weekend-essay/why-ai-isnt-going-to-make-art
42. Stanley, K. O. & Lehman, J. (2015). *Why Greatness Cannot Be Planned: The Myth of the Objective*. Springer.
43. Buntz, B. July 24, 2023. "Sanofi Puts AI 'Plai' App at the Center of Drug Discovery and Clinical Trial Operations." *Drug Discovery and Development*. https://www.drugdiscoverytrends.com/sanofi-ai-drug-development/
44. Sport Conrad. February 18, 2022. "On: From Garden Hose to Sports Innovation." *Sport Conrad Blog*. https://www.sport-conrad.com/blog/en/on-from-garden-hose-to-sports-innovation/
45. Lindkvist, M. (2016). *Minifesto: Why Small Ideas Matter in the World of Grand Narratives*. LID Publishing
46. Stanley, K. O. & Lehman, J. (2015). *Why Greatness Cannot Be Planned: The Myth of the Objective*. Springer
47. Koestler, A. (1964). *The Act of Creation*. Hutchinson
48. United Nations. (n.d.). Dag Hammarskjöld: 1955. United Nations. https://www.un.org/depts/dhl/dag/time1955.htm
49. Spiegelhalter, D. (2024). *The Art of Uncertainty: How to Navigate Chance, Ignorance, Risk, and Luck*. Pelican. Pages 3 and 5

50. Proust, M. (n.d.). The Madeleine (Excerpt from *Remembrance of Things Past*). *DailyGood*. https://www.dailygood.org/story/2136/the-madeleine-excerpt-from-remembrance-of-things-past-marcel-proust/

51. A common acronym used on social media when an article is 'Too Long, Didn't Read' and, therefore, requires a two-sentence summary

52. Kestin, G. et al. (2024). "AI Tutoring Outperforms Active Learning." *Research Square*. https://doi.org/10.21203/rs.3.rs-4243877/v1

53. De Simone, M. E. et al. September 18, 2024. "From Chalkboards to Chatbots in Nigeria: 7 Lessons to Pioneer Generative AI for Education." *World Bank Blogs*. https://blogs.worldbank.org/en/education/From-chalkboards-to-chatbots-in-Nigeria

54. Personal interview with David Dixon conducted on February 11, 2025

55. Mollick, E. February 15, 2024. [Post on *X*]. Retrieved from https://x.com/emollick/status/1891913605890609624

56. Walsh, D. January 30, 2024. "A New Look at the Economics of AI." *MIT Sloan Ideas Made to Matter*. https://mitsloan.mit.edu/ideas-made-to-matter/a-new-look-economics-ai

57. Burn-Murdoch, J. March 28, 2025. "Why Hasn't AI Taken Your Job Yet?" *Financial Times*

58. Frey, C. B. & Osborne, M. A. (2023). Generative AI and the Future of Work: A Reappraisal. Retrieved from https://oms-www.files.svdcdn.com/production/downloads/academic/2023-FoW-Working-Paper-Generative-AI-and-the-Future-of-Work-A-Reappraisal-combined.pdf

59. Slack (Salesforce). (2024). The Fall 2024 Workforce Index Shows AI Hype is Cooling. Retrieved from https://slack.com/blog/news/the-fall-2024-workforce-index-shows-ai-hype-is-cooling

60. NTT DATA. (2024). Global GenAI Report: How Organizations Are Mastering Their GenAI Destiny in 2025. Retrieved from https://us.nttdata.com/en/-/media/NTTDataAmerica/Files/gated-asset/NTT-DATA-Global-GenAI-Report.pdf

61. Thompson, C. February 22, 2023. "The Risk of a New AI Winter." *Medium*. https://clivethompson.medium.com/the-risk-of-a-new-ai-winter-332ffb4767f0

62. McKinsey & Company. June 14, 2022. "Value Creation in the Metaverse." *McKinsey & Company*. Retrieved June 17, 2025, from https://www.mckinsey.com/capabilities/growth-marketing-and-sales/our-insights/value-creation-in-the-metaverse

ENDNOTES

63. Goh, E. et al (2024). "Large Language Model Influence on Diagnostic Reasoning: A Randomized Clinical Trial." *JAMA Network Open*, 7(10), e2440969. https://doi.org/10.1001/jamanetworkopen.2024.40969

64. Litt, D. (2024). "AI-generated Mathematical Research? Not So Fast." [Post on *X*]. https://x.com/littmath/status/1891868756340547809?s=43

65. World Health Organization. (2018). "International Classification of Diseases 11th Revision (ICD-11): 6C51 Gaming disorder." *World Health Organization*. https://icd.who.int/browse11/l-m/en#/http://id.who.int/icd/entity/1448597234

66. Mollick, E. (2024). "Why Doesn't Anyone Check?" [Post on *X*]. https://x.com/emollick/status/1891385342592249856

67. *The Economist*. (2025). "How AI Will Divide The Best From The Rest." https://www.economist.com/finance-and-economics/2025/02/13/how-ai-will-divide-the-best-from-the-rest

68. "AltaVista." Wikipedia. https://en.wikipedia.org/wiki/AltaVista

69. Sull, D. N. (1999). "Why Good Companies Go Bad." *Harvard Business Review*, 77(4), 42-52. https://pubmed.ncbi.nlm.nih.gov/10539208/

70. "What Happened to AltaVista? The Rise and Fall of a Search Pioneer." *EM360Tech*, July 12, 2024. https://em360tech.com/tech-articles/what-happened-altavista-rise-and-fall-search-pioneer

71. Henn, S. November 6, 2023. "The Whole Earth Catalog Was The Internet Before The Internet." *NPR*. https://www.npr.org/2023/11/06/1210826844/the-whole-earth-catalog-was-the-internet-before-the-internet

72. Many points on this list were originally made by Chris Alvino. [Post on *X*]. https://x.com/ChrisAlvino/status/1804823161076080887.

73. *The New York Times*. "Authors Sue OpenAI and Meta Over Copyright Infringement." August 2024

74. Frermann, L. & Cohney, S. February 15, 2024. "OpenAI Says DeepSeek Inappropriately Copied ChatGPT – But It's Facing Copyright Claims Too." *The Conversation*. https://theconversation.com/openai-says-deepseek-inappropriately-copied-chatgpt-but-its-facing-copyright-claims-too-248863

75. *Fortune*. "ChatGPT Produces the Same Amount of CO_2 Emissions as 260 Flights." January 21, 2025. https://fortune.com/2025/01/21/chatgpt-carbon-dioxide-emissions-study/

76. MIT Sloan. (n.d.). "When AI Gets It Wrong: Addressing AI Hallucinations and Bias." *MIT Sloan Educational Technology Office*. https://mitsloanedtech.mit.edu/ai/basics/addressing-ai-hallucinations-and-bias/

77. Bond, S. May 14, 2024. "AI-generated Spam is Starting to Fill Social Media. Here's Why." *NPR*. https://www.npr.org/2024/05/14/1251072726/ai-spam-images-facebook-linkedin-threads-meta

78. Viola, K. (2024). "'Another Body' Documentary Exposes Harm of Deepfake technology." *Cornell University*. https://sts.cornell.edu/news/another-body-documentary-exposes-harm-deepfake-technology

79. Spall, V. May 20, 2024. "Google Rolls Out AI in SERPs in the US – and Everyone Hates it." *Browser Media*. https://browsermedia.agency/blog/google-rolls-out-ai-in-serps-in-the-us-and-everyone-hates-it/

80. Adobe Care. (n.d.). Adobe Support Community. https://community.adobe.com/t5/acrobat-discussions/why-are-you-adding-ai-when-acrobat-et-al-is-a-dumpster-fire/m-p/14908803

81. Greyling, C. February 21, 2024. "Catastrophic Forgetting in LLMs." *Medium*. https://cobusgreyling.medium.com/catastrophic-forgetting-in-llms-bf345760e6e2

82. Taylor, J. December 1, 2023. "Making a Large Language Model Transparent, Compliant, and Reliable." *Forbes*. https://www.forbes.com/councils/forbesbusinesscouncil/2023/12/01/making-a-large-language-model-transparent-compliant-and-reliable/

83. Sánchez Salido, E. et al. (2025). "None of the Others: A General Technique to Distinguish Reasoning from Memorization in Multiple-Choice LLM Evaluation Benchmarks." *arXiv*. https://doi.org/10.48550/arXiv.2502.12896

84. Mollick, E. (2024). *Co-intelligence: Living and Working with AI*. Portfolio

85. Parson, E. June 1, 2001. "The 1910s (1910–1919)." *EC&M*. https://www.ecmweb.com/content/article/20885877/the-1910s-1910-1919

86. Peng, S. et al. (2023). "The Impact of AI on Developer Productivity: Evidence from GitHub Copilot." *arXiv preprint arXiv:2302.06590*

ENDNOTES

87. Brown, L. (2024). "New Research Reveals AI Coding Assistants Boost Developer Productivity by 26%: What IT Leaders Need to Know." *IT Revolution.* https://itrevolution.com/articles/new-research-reveals-ai-coding-assistants-boost-developer-productivity-by-26-what-it-leaders-need-to-know/

88. Brynjolfsson, E. et al. (2024). "Generative AI at Work." *The Quarterly Journal of Economics.* https://doi.org/10.1093/qje/qjae044

89. Noy, S. & Zhang, W. (2023). "Experimental Evidence on the Productivity Effects of Generative Artificial Intelligence." *Science*

90. Chen, Z. & Chan, J. (2024). "Large Language Model in Creative Work: The Role of Collaboration Modality and User Expertise." *Management Science, 70*(12). https://doi.org/10.1287/mnsc.2023.03014

91. Choi, J. H. et al. (2024). "Lawyering in the Age of Artificial Intelligence." *Minnesota Law Review, 109* (Forthcoming). *Minnesota Legal Studies Research Paper No. 23-31*

92. Otis, N. et al. (2024). "The Uneven Impact of Generative AI on Entrepreneurial Performance." *SSRN.* https://papers.ssrn.com/sol3/papers.cfm?abstract_id=4671369

93. Roldán-Monés, A. et al. (2024). "When GenAI Increases Inequality: Evidence from a University Debating Competition." *Esade.* https://www.esade.edu/ecpol/wp-content/uploads/2019/09/2409-ChatGPTRoldan_ecpol.pdf

94. Kim, H. et al. (2024). "AI, Investment Decisions, and Inequality." *SSRN*

95. Transforming Transportation Advisory Committee. (2024). *Formal Recommendations of the Transforming Transportation Advisory Committee to the US Department of Transportation on Artificial Intelligence, Automated Driving, Project Delivery, and Innovation for Safety.* Retrieved from https://downloads.regulations.gov/DOT-OST-2024-0124-0002/attachment_1.pdf

96. Moravec's paradox refers to the observation that tasks humans find effortless—like perception, movement, or common sense—are often the hardest for AI, while tasks that seem intellectually complex—like playing chess or solving equations—can be relatively easy for machines. It highlights how evolution has made our 'simple' abilities deeply sophisticated.

97. Payne, A. (2021). *Built to Fail: The Inside Story of Blockbuster's Inevitable Bust.* Lioncrest Publishing

98. Law Commission. (n.d.). *Automated Vehicles.* https://lawcom.gov.uk/project/automated-vehicles/

99. Cahn, D. June 20, 2024. "AI's $600B question." *Sequoia Capital.* https://www.sequoiacap.com/article/ais-600b-question/
100. These examples and an inspirational longer list from https://patrickcollison.com/fast
101. Flyvbjerg, B. & Gardner, B. (2023). *How Big Things Get Done: The Surprising Factors That Determine the Fate of Every Project, from Home Renovations to Space Exploration and Everything In Between.* Currency
102. Financial Times. February 28, 2025. "Political Scientist Bjorn Lomborg: 'You Can't Spend on Everything'." *Lunch with the FT.* https://www.ft.com/content/fb51285a-9102-4640-9838-f998d00cde94
103. Freedom House. (n.d.). "Freedom in the World: Country Scores and Status." *Freedom House.* Retrieved June 17, 2025, from https://freedomhouse.org/countries/freedom-world/scores?sort=desc&order=Total%20Score%20and%20Status
104. Saxenian, A. (1994). *Regional Advantage: Culture and Competition in Silicon Valley and Route 128.* Harvard University Press
105. Greenspan, A., & Wooldridge, A. (2018). *Capitalism in America: A History.* Page 179, Penguin Press
106. Ritchie, H. March 6, 2023. "China Uses as Much Cement in Two Years as the US Did Over the Entire 20th Century." *Sustainability by Numbers.* https://www.sustainabilitybynumbers.com/p/china-us-cement
107. McLuhan coined the term 'global village' in *The Gutenberg Galaxy: The Making of Typographic Man* (1962) and later expanded on the concept in *Understanding Media: The Extensions of Man* (1964)
108. Our World in Data. (n.d.). Trust in State Institutions (World Values Survey), 2022 [Data Visualization]. *Global Change Data Lab.* Retrieved June 17, 2025, from https://ourworldindata.org/grapher/trust-state-institutions-wvs?time=2022
109. Labbé, T. (2025, March 3). The Surreal Exchange Between Trump and Zelensky Objectively Seemed to Me Like a Victory of Falsehood and Brutality Over Truth and Diplomacy. *LinkedIn*
110. Walker Smith, B. (2019, November 14). *The Trustworthy Automated Driving Company* [PowerPoint slides]. Newly Possible
111. Hobart, B. & Huber, T. *Boom: Bubbles and the End of Stagnation* (South San Francisco, CA: Stripe Press, 2024), Page 265

ENDNOTES

112. Barlow, J. P. February 8, 1996. "A Declaration of the Independence of Cyberspace." *Electronic Frontier Foundation*. https://www.eff.org/cyberspace-independence

113. Nordhaus, W. D. (1997). Do real-output and real-wage measures capture reality? The history of lighting suggests not. In T. F. Bresnahan & R. J. Gordon (Eds.), *The economics of new goods* (pp. 29–66). University of Chicago Press. https://lucept.com/wp-content/uploads/2014/11/william-nordhaus-the-cost-of-light.pdf

114. Confino, P. January 17, 2025. "Goldman Sachs CEO says that AI can draft 95% of an IPO prospectus in minutes." *Fortune*. https://fortune.com/2025/01/17/goldman-sachs-ceo-david-solomon-ai-tasks-ipo-prospectus-s1-filing-sec/

115. Chris Nashawaty. *The Future Was Now: Madmen, Mavericks, and the Epic Sci-Fi Summer of 1982* (Flatiron Books, 2024), 42–43.

116. Evans, C. L. April 3, 2013. "OMNI: The Forgotten History of The Best Science Magazine That Ever Was." *VICE*. Retrieved June 17, 2025, from https://www.vice.com/en/article/omni-the-forgotten-history-of-the-best-science-magazine-that-ever-was

117. Liang, W. et al. (2025). "The Widespread Adoption of Large Language Model-assisted Writing Across Society." *arXiv*. https://doi.org/10.48550/arXiv.2502.09747

118. Shapiro, D. December 2, 2024. "The 'I just realized how huge AI is.'" *Substack*. https://daveshap.substack.com/p/the-i-just-realized-how-huge-ai-is

119. An acronym for the five stages of grief she proposed: Denial, Anger, Bargaining, Depression, and Acceptance.

120. LeCun, Y. [@ylecun]. April 22, 2023. "The AI Systems of the Future Will Not Be Stochastic Parrots. They Will Understand the World Like Humans Do." [Post on X]. https://x.com/ylecun/status/1649670485498822656

121. Marchese, D. January 18, 2025. "Curtis Yarvin Says Democracy is Done. Powerful Conservatives are Listening." *The New York Times*

122. SIL International's *Ethnologue: Languages of the World*

123. BUILD OR DIE. [@BUILD_OR_DIE]. (2024, September 17). [Post on X.] https://x.com/BUILD_OR_DIE/status/1773570462016020960. It also brings to mind one of the picket signs during the Hollywood's Writer's Strike in 2023: "ChatGPT does not have childhood trauma."

ACKNOWLEDGMENTS

Thank you to the following people for contributing valuable input and suggestions to our book:

Mauricio Muñoz
Gregory Neiswander
Christopher Tassone
Bruce Mehler
Björn Jeffery
Fredrik Härén
Fredrik Laurell
Ola Bostrom
Mats Nordlund
David Dixon
William Oliver